Torn Between
My Love for
GOD&GAYS

JOE N. BROWN SR.

Torn Between
My Love for
GOD&GAYS

TATE PUBLISHING
AND ENTERPRISES, LLC

Published by Tate Publishing & Enterprises, LLC
127 E. Trade Center Terrace | Mustang, Oklahoma 73064 USA
1.888.361.9473 | www.tatepublishing.com

Tate Publishing is committed to excellence in the publishing industry. The company reflects the philosophy established by the founders, based on Psalm 68:11,
"The Lord gave the word and great was the company of those who published it."

Book design copyright © 2016 by Tate Publishing, LLC. All rights reserved.
Cover design by Jeffrey Doblados
Interior design by Gram Telen

Published in the United States of America
ISBN: 978-1-68097-966-4
Religion / Christian Life / Social Issues
15.11.13

Acknowledgments

I would like the world to know how hard my wife, Neecha M. Jackson-Brown, worked on this project in the entry of data for this book. It is because of her dedication and hard work with this novel that we were able to complete it. She spent thousands of hours working, typing, proofreading, and editing without any pay. My wife's belief in me, her faith and belief in God, her thirty-six years of support for my dreams, and her tireless efforts in helping me obtain my dreams is why I consider her an angel of God. The importance of this message and the completion of this book was made possible by her efforts.

I would like to thank my sister Recheal Stewart-Brown and my sister-in-law Lisa Stewart-Brown, whose relationships with with my family and I have allowed me to mature in my view of homosexuality and who have inspired me and demonstrated their unconditional love for me and my family. I also thank them for their much-needed support of my writings and my books. For this and many other things, I will always love them both. I would also like to acknowledge my sister Rene Brown and my sister-in-law Julie, who are mentioned in this book. Because of our family ties, I will always love, treasure, value, and maintain the hope of a better tomorrow for our relationship.

I would also like to acknowledge my other brothers and sisters and their spouses who are and have always been a part of my life and whom I dearly love. Wilbern (Veronica) aka Bishop Brown, Jr.; Patricia (Jay) Jackson; Tony (Cynthia) Brown; Randy (Mieke) Brown; Cecelia Brown; and Tyrone. Brother-in-law

Don (Sharon) Allen and a special recognition from my wife's niece Rugenia Dickens for her support.

Thanks to all my children and nineteen-plus grandchildren for your love and support. Without your presence in my life, I would not be able to have the pride and confidence to write as I do and to feel as blessed as I am.

My children:

Daughter: Keeshondra Brown-Walton	Son-in-law: Bakari Walton
Son: Nathen Q. Brown	Daughter-in-law: Krystle Wicks-Brown
Daughter: Joneika Brown-Williams	Son-in-law: Jermaine Williams
Son: Damu R. Brown	Daughter-in-law: Heidi Daniels
Daughter: J. Shani Brown	Son: J. Tyreece Brown
Son: Joe N. Brown Jr.	Daughter-in-law: Tammy Brown
Sister: Donna Collins-Williams	Brother-in-law: Ricky Williams Sr.

Contents

Introduction

You are now reading this book's introduction. Perhaps the title *God* and *Gays* have stirred your curiosity and stimulated you to question what this book may be saying. In fact, you might feel that these two words together is a symbol of our social divide over homosexuality, and you might also agree that this subject has become the center of controversy—not only in our society but all over the world as well. Now you anticipate to find what this writer's opinion is about the subject of God and gays.

As the author, my inspiration to share my experience took flight out of the passion for my religion and was propelled by my desire to share what I felt and experienced after discovering that my sisters and other relatives were gay. As a son of a preacher, the influence came upon me to think that religion and those who believe in it should be the example of how we should treat others. Also, it was taught that God is love and that He cares for all his creation. But it appeared to me that those who are religious do not often consider homosexuals as being part of their religious institutions, and this began to bother me over time. Fortunately, as a result of seeing things this way, it helped me to better understand how and why we are so divided in society over this subject.

My journey began as a result of finding out that my sisters were gay. When their homosexual relationships became noticeable and upon realizing this, one of my first interests was wanting to know exactly how this was against our religion and our traditions. I wanted to use my research on this subject as a tactic to help in my pursuit of condemning them for their homosexuality. These thoughts started my guilt and also confirmed how I had gone too far in my opposition of how they lived their life. As time passed, it became more obvious to me how most people felt and what they thought about gays in our society. It seemed that people who were religious were much worse in their negative opinion of homosexuals compared to anyone else. At my church, it was normal for me to go to other members and ask them to collectively pray for my problems. However, announcing to them that my family members were homosexuals and asking the church for prayer for those reasons made me afraid and embarrassed of exposing my family's dark secrets. This was the first of my many encounters with religious people and their prejudice against homosexuality. I started to feel that most of them had little concern for the souls of people who are homosexuals. Also, even if I were to ask for their help, I'm not certain as to what kind of assistance anyone at my church could have provided other than their prayers for something that they felt morally against. However, despite this, I thought that knowing that someone is concerned for your well-being can be very important to someone.

Over time, the homosexuality choice of my sisters became a dividing weapon for my family, our religion, and my faith. It has challenged our family's beliefs and interpretation of what the Creator's laws are for us, and because of this, the questions of whether these biblical expectations are really that of man or from our divine Father is what became significant to me. Also, it was clear from this belief that my relationship with my sisters and the doctrine of the religion that I believed in were now under conflict. It seemed but logical to think that to expect to have everything the way it was before was no longer realistic. It felt as if there were no other options left for me to consider that were acceptable.

My problem was that my passion for wanting to be loyal to my religion was almost as strong as my desire to maintain the relationships that I had with my sisters. In addition to that, I did not have enough understanding at that time of how our Creator expects his followers to treat homosexuals. It was difficult for me to feel satisfied with condemning anyone as a way to solve my problem. I was committed to applying what I learned from the teachings of our faith that required us to love each other and to forgive one another. Also, I was taught that the Bible warns mankind that judgment of others is God's alone. Because of this, it became difficult for me to understand how believers of a religion (the foundation of which was love) could treat gay people in a way contrary to what they believed in.

I felt it was important to be correct in the way my thinking was about homosexuals. However, in order to find exactly what my religion's position was on this subject required me to undergo an intensive biblical research, specifically for any evidence of what the Bible requires and His expectations for how we treat others that are this way. However, trying to get a balanced opinion from members of religious authority and getting the right information about the subject from an impartial opinion is what essentially became most challenging for me. When researching for facts on this subject, I discovered that everyone had their different views. However, it was difficult for me to agree with most people and their points of view, because after consideration of everything that I had learned on this subject, my feelings were that most religious believers' feelings about homosexuals were of extreme hatred. Their views always seemed to lack consideration of the entire facts that should form the basis of their opinions. It appeared to me that there is evidence to support the belief that most people's negative opinions, which are based on their biblical laws about homosexuality, are influenced by our traditions and beliefs, as opposed to what God's laws actually are. When trying to understand the reasons for many people's mind-sets, it eventually became obvious to me that their hatred for homosexuals in itself is against our religious practices.

I feel that when we are torn between our religion and homosexuality, it is evident when we are confused and can't commit to any opinion. Also, it's when our thoughts are in between the two extremes of accepting or not accepting homosexuality. From this, some may think that they have taken a less controversial position and that their thinking equally opposes both sides, while at the same time, it is equally accepting of both views. It is as if we won't commit ourselves to either point of view that is *for* or *against* homosexuality equality.

This book explains how I dealt with my anger over my sisters' homosexuality and describes how I evolved throughout my life. It also enumerates the reasons why it changed and how it developed me into who I am today. As a direct result of this, my readers learn from this information and how this process was for me in accepting their choice to live their life and how I evolved with years of anger. I also elaborate on the way religion has worked to help me better understand how homosexuality affects people who are straight as well as those that are gay. My readers become educated about the reasons why these expectations from God to love everyone equally are intended for all mankind to follow. Also, it provides different scriptures that imply how He requires the entire world to do the same.

Part of this book's message reflects back to the time in society when "homosexuality equality" was in its early stages of development, and from this, we learn how difficult it was then for those who were gay to express their views. With this information, we also begin to realize why our religious community is now experiencing such great opposition against its beliefs about homosexuality, especially from the victims who have been the target of our religious condemnation.

After reading this book, my readers will ultimately learn from my good and bad experiences in adjusting to the homosexuality in my family. This story is explained from a unique point of view as a result of my experiences of life and using my in-depth understanding of Scripture. The book's message takes the position that our traditions and beliefs have gotten in the way of us evolving into what our Creator actually intended us to be. Much of this developed thinking are perspectives that I've learned from religious leaders and followers throughout my life. My message will reveal what many religious people actually think privately about homosexuality. This book exposes the inner thinking of many religious people who normally would not truthfully expose to others how they felt.

My story exemplifies just how our religious traditions have evolved into the present barriers that our society and world faces today when it comes to accepting homosexuals within its religious body. It provides the reasons why this is a result of most religious followers' lack of knowledge of the Bible. This book will illustrate the different ways that religion has dealt with homosexuality in past cultures and remind us of the barbaric methods that were used in the religious condemnation of people in history. Within this book, examples are given as to why that relates with our society today. The hope is that all who read this might become aware of the unsuccessful methods in the way I treated people when I used religion as a way to condemn others. As a result of explaining this, my readers will also discover the realities of what I encountered while adjusting to the homosexuality of my family and their life partners.

This book allows my readers to understand my experiences when I was seeking the way to become normal again after discovering that my sisters were gay. My readers will be exposed to points of views of what others actually think and feel after they have discovered that someone they know is homosexual, whom they previously thought was straight. My objective is to explain the mistakes we often make when we attempt to change the life and views of others. From this information, we are empowered to be more prepared for the future problems we encounter. I make the point that when we are trying to change someone's views—whether their opinions are *for* or *against* homosexuality equality—and in doing so how it will have a negative impact on everyone's lives.

The hope is that my readers will begin to understand how, despite our good intentions, our opposition and expectations for the way people live their lives are potentially hurtful to all of those who are involved. In fact, whether we admit this fact or not, there are many relationships that are divided over homosexuality and religion, and often, these are relationships that most of us once valued. The hope is that we learn that there are consequences from our failure to be compassionate in our views of others. By doing this, it is more likely that we can restore our relationship with those that we were close to.

In this book, my primary objectives are to convince my readers that we gain nothing when we condemn each other through our different beliefs and traditions and explaining how we must be aware of the results from our actions. In fact, I have dedicated an entire chapter in this book explaining the different ways that we usually become critical of each other and why we have done this since the beginning of society. This chapter's topics will highlight examples of the way man has always condemned others and justified his actions through his religious traditions and beliefs. It also gives explanations for why most of the things that we believe in religion are borne out of our different beliefs and traditions. This chapter attempts to make the point of how our history is a link in the way we view things today and why these influences often start in our school system, beginning with teachers comparing our scores with other students as well as the way we compete with each other in our school sports and at home with our game shows and Internet connections. Also, how we use our homes, cars, and jewelry as a symbol of our sense of superiority over others. I connect these points with how religion has judgment of us, and from this we learn of the similarities within this book and the subjects of religion and homosexuality.

My readers are engaged in a way that helps us realize the realities of our behavior patterns that have led to how we condemn others today. It seems to me that whether we are religious or not, homosexual or straight, we all have expectations of how we feel everyone should think or act as well as how other people should live. What we expect of others is something that is learned from our society, and it is justified by our traditions and beliefs that are designed to pass judgment on others.

Within this book, my readers will learn from my unique experience of being the son of a preacher as well as gain knowledge about homosexuality and religion from that learned perspective. My story gives a unique consideration about both subjects, and it provides a different view for my readers with real-life examples of how most religious followers think and feel about homosexuality. The significant tool that has helped influence my writing about this subject is my passionate desire to share with the world my belief that the creation of our religious views on many different issues are influenced by our traditions, which often lack the biblical facts to support these views. In fact, one of this books' chapters gives examples from personal experiences with religious followers and leaders, all coming from different denominations and beliefs making a point of how impossible it can be in not only just finding out facts about the reasons for our traditions of the religion that we believe in, but also the difficulties we incur in learning how to love religious people. This chapter helps us to understand how we are all unique, and from this we realize that we are often divided by our different traditions and beliefs, which was passed down to us. Despite this, we share the same Creator, which is God. However, learning to love most religious people who openly express hatred, especially those who feel that they are entitled to express their critical views based on their religion, is what this book shall explore in the chapter called "Learning to Love Religious People."

After learning about my sisters' homosexuality and investigating certain aspects of my belief, I began to believe that for religious followers to develop a hostile thinking of homosexuals, it would be because they did not know or care about biblical facts. In this chapter, I will explain the common thinking of most religious followers. By doing so, readers can understand their reasons for having their beliefs about homosexuality. From this, we can better understand why those who have this belief condemn not just homosexuality, but rather how the history itself of religion have always enforced its condemnation on a wide range of other traditions and belief of what was thought by them to be the things God expects from mankind.

Ultimately, I hope that my readers can begin to understand these topics of interest which suggest that those who believe in religion are just simply followers of a belief of a particular religion and of the traditions from that religion. I'm actually presenting facts that there is no one alive today that was present in that day and time to personally witness God establishing the laws for mankind or creating things in our world. Also, there is no one alive today that was there to witness Jesus Christ walk on this earth, and there certainly isn't anyone today who was able to meet and talk with those who wrote the books of the Bible, who are still alive today. I'm trying to illustrate the point that those who believe in religion all believe in the history of a religion based upon little facts, if any at all. Readers will learn from the perspectives of those who believe in God in a way that others might feel uncomfortable revealing. This subject will identify the present challenges that our religion faces today when dealing with homosexuality. In fact, this book reveals the different reasons why religion and its followers are sometimes out of touch with the way God requires us to love. This book discusses the many methods of condemnation that have been used by leaders and followers. With this, I make a point of how our religion and some of its people have developed a lack of understanding of whom and how we should love, and a misunderstanding of God and what His expectations are for mankind.

This book illustrates how some religious people and their leaders have led people with its critiquing and derogation of them while lusting in its self-pride, rather than making it their priority in finding a way to help and teach others. This book reveals that there are religious believers and nonbelievers, homosexuals and straight people, that are all seeking to learn who our Creator is and how to love Him. Throughout this novel, scriptures are used to support my position that God is love and that it is because of this that He has always allowed His creation the freedom of choice. In my arguments that are supported with these scriptures, readers will find that the example He has paved for mankind to follow is that of Jesus Christ, which is to treat everyone we meet with love as He did.

In the chapter titled "Learning How to Love God," my readers will learn about the different barriers that commonly prevent most of us from learning who our Creator is. The book demonstrates this by showing how some of these divisions influence us to believe things a certain way within our culture, our families, and our religious traditions. Also, this illustrates how some of our distrust against the Almighty can begin from worldly disasters that have affected us or from the death of those we loved, and as a result we may have blamed God. There are other examples that explain other reasons that we may be at fault in learning how to love others without knowing it. In this particular chapter, I expose how finding the way to do this for some in the world is not as easy or as simple to identify as most may assume. However, the facts presented in this book will educate and inform my readers as they learn from my life experiences and the way I dealt with religion and homosexuality. This book's message will inform readers how it's possible that some religious leaders and followers are still developing in their understanding of religion and that most of us are evolving in learning how to love others as God has commanded us, whether we are religious or not.

The chapter titled "Learning How to Love Gays" explains why many religious followers are in need of learning how to love gays as well as how and why many of them are often criticized for not doing so. I make the point that most religious followers know and practice what the fundamental aspects of what love is for others from what we were taught; but actually are still evolving in learning how to love themselves, as well as caring for all others in this world and while doing this, still evolving in their learning to know our Creator. In this chapter, this story will educate my readers about homosexuality and religion, especially those who have difficulty accepting the concept of it mixing within our society and our religion. I'm sure that for some, this idea may seem insulting, but the reality is that most religious followers and leaders *do* need to elaborate more about this subject. To me, it's clear that part of learning how to love gays could require those who do this start by understanding that God requires us to love everyone and that not doing this would be against what He intended for his followers.

Within this book, I will go on to explain how when we have such compassion for others that we otherwise would not. As a consequence of this, there are health benefits for the presenter who does this, as well as the internal satisfaction we obtain as a result of having done this for others. We began to learn from the fact that when we judge ourselves, and use that as our examples in our expectation of how to live from this, and with this information we learn that it can be used as our tool in finding a source of tolerance for the way others live. It's obvious to me that if we assess ourselves, it will result in us becoming more aware of our faults, and it will reveal to us many different things about ourselves that will make us believe we are in need of a change of thinking, instead of others needing this. It will actually help us discover how we are struggling ourselves over the same things that what we accuse others of. Our weaknesses and shortcomings begin to magnify themselves to us as a direct result of our self-analytical view. If we do this, then with time we will better understand why God requires that we are to love all His creation, and we will understand more clearly the reason He requires mankind not to judge others unless we ourselves might be judged. While living by these standards over time, we begin to grow and mature in our views of many things, including homosexuality.

From this, we begin to have a deeper appreciation for others and a better understanding of our imperfections. This eventually serves as the pathway for our growth. But for us to be successful at this, we must have respect for everyone—gay or straight. We must be motivated to care for others who challenge us and our values, so that we truly can say that we are followers of a belief in compassion for others. Jesus Himself, in the Bible, is seen many times defending people against religious condemnation and persecution. Jesus is even quoted as saying, "Whoever is without sin, may they cast the first stone" when a mob was about to stone to death a woman who had committed adultery. Jesus Christ has proven that He Himself is the example of man's religious persecution as a result of Him being falsely accused. He is also the example of why learning how to have compassion for gays in our society is necessary for us as followers of a God of love. Those that won't adhere to this is an example of our failure to teach this as a religious institution as well as our failure as individuals to do what God expects of us, which is to love everyone as we would ourselves. Essentially, we learn that God is love, and our challenge on Earth is learning to have compassion for all others despite who they are. From our pursuit of these feelings for others, we realize that we are more able to discover peace and harmony with people when we are noncritical of them.

Pope Francis made a major statement in August 2013. His message was televised on CNN News and on other major networks. The Pope is quoted as saying that "the lives of homosexuals and homosexual priest are not for him to judge, only God." As the writer of *Torn between My Love for God and Gays*, my story also recognizes that God's purpose for the creation of mankind is for us to have the ability of freedom of choice and that He doesn't force us to have religion in our lives; neither does the Almighty require mankind to judge others on His behalf. In fact, in the Bible, He has warned mankind that judgment is his job alone.

I believe that our desire to follow our religion should be reason enough to help promote all of us in reserving our judgment of others as well as reasons to influence us to search for a way to care for others unconditionally, and allow the Almighty to have the final judgment for all of us—not mankind. I believe we will get there when we are aware that we ourselves are not perfect, and we may realize this about ourselves after searching and finding the truth that exists within us.

1

Religions That Fail to Love All

During my early childhood, I had no knowledge about homosexuality. I would later discover that members of my own family were gay. Soon after this newfound knowledge, it caused a conflict between my religion and them. Because of that, it became to be one of the most important issues for me to understand—which is, finding out why our religion and traditions are opposed to homosexuality. For me, this also became a quest to better understand God and His laws for us. In my early adulthood, I began to be aware that there were some people who felt that religion and homosexuality did not mix together. However, I concluded that homosexuals deserve to worship just like all others who are straight, and I felt that they need the support from our religious leaders in finding a personal relationship with religion. I thought because of all that I had faced in the past that if this were me being treated this way, how hard it would have been to find my peace in religion as I have done. It was surprising to me that no one had a reasonable explanation that could justify why the consideration for people's souls is only available for selected people. To me, it's noticeable that there are those that are being neglected by these institutions and that these are people who are in need of their help, the same as others that are normally helped.

Throughout the years, I've discovered that most religious followers, even with their good intentions, still maintain expectations for how others live. For example, when our beliefs and traditions are different from others', we're likely to feel a disconnection with them. By nature, we feel out of our comfort zone when there is someone who's different or doesn't share our values. It is a pattern in our behavior that exists and that most of us might not be aware of. This is an example of how sometimes our opinions of people can be a method of victimizing those who we falsely prejudge. The questions that we should eventually consider are these: When does our suspicion of others become considered as paranoia? How can we accurately gauge when we have developed unfair opinions of others? Perhaps this might require us to analyze our motives for why we think this way. From this, we may receive a better understanding as to why we do what we do.

There are some who believe that with their prayers they'll always have God's forgiveness for the things they do, and so they operate with an overabundant sense of security in their expectations of the Almighty. What I'm saying is that most of us that do believe by our asking for His forgiveness, that we think everything is always forgiven by Him, which is possible! However, this can sometimes bring out the arrogance in our thinking. Some may come to the conclusion that they have a more exclusive right than others or that they have a free pass to hurt others because we can pray after we go against the laws of our belief. My belief is that our ability to pray can give us this false sense of entitlement with religion. Some may think that because they participate in worship service while others may not, this makes them more qualified at religion than others. Some of us might condemn those that are not part of our religion or that practice traditions that we do not agree with. Most of us are in denial about what we do and are unaware of its effectiveness to hurt people. It seems for some people, their original intentions for belief in religion over time changes and redevelops in us using our belief in religion as an instrument to hide the things we don't want the world to see about ourselves, or using it as a way to reveal things for the world to see about others. Some might use this tactic to fulfill a sense of closeness to religion or God for themselves.

I wrote this chapter so that my readers are able to better understand how we overcome life's many issues that conflict with us as we attempt to live out our traditions and beliefs and for others to understand how religious leaders and believers are sometimes unsuccessful in their attempt to live life according to their message, making a point that it's likely God is perfect and what He created is perfect, but mankind is not always accurate in what we believe and teach. Because of our different beliefs in religion, our traditions will continue to reshape itself and its influence in what we believe in the future.

Since my early adulthood, I always thought that those who believed in God loved everyone. It was disturbing for me to discover that there were people that hated others as the religious world hates homosexuality. I have always considered the church as a hospital for sick souls, and it did not really matter to me what one was sick of, only that they needed to be healed. As a religious believer and as one who loves God, it later became clear to me that a solution for this problem had become essential. As an institution, we must not allow our example to be about how we judge others. Rather, it should represent how we have compassion for others, and we should allow our judgment and opinions to be left in the control of our God, who is love.

Mankind's inability to comprehend how God is able to have love for all those who believe in him and also those that don't has puzzled most believers and nonbelievers of religion, particularly over the interpretation of His Word in which the Almighty describes what He dislikes in the lives of mankind. It seems that this is part of what causes our being confused in the interpretation of what God meant in that passage in the Bible and the expectation of how we should treat others that are homosexual. However, mankind's condemnation upon others for the way they live is usually supported by our religious traditions and belief, and when this is done, it can be compared with those who crucified Jesus Christ. Those involved felt they were demonstrating commitment to their belief by killing Jesus. This was from their fear that turned to hatred, which ultimately led to His death.

Today, what we believe from what was learned from our religions and their traditions are as the results of thousands of years of how our ancestors dealt with homosexuality. Despite our religious beliefs, there are religious leaders who have been found guilty of enormous wrongdoings, contrary to what they have represented. Because of this and an enormous amount of other claims and also the way religion has dealt with homosexuality in the past, a rebellious revolution was borne that is led by homosexuals and their activists in an attempt to fight against any social unfairness that threatens homosexuality equality. It appears that they have already dealt an almost lethal blow to those who oppose their rights for equality.

There have been many religious leaders that have judged others for so long and now have been found to be hypocritical. They have given reasons to believers and unbelievers to question the legitimacy of religion and its followers. Most are wondering how anyone guilty of these types of wrongdoings can be so bold as to judge another, especially when it is our leaders. In fact, most justify that they're turning away from religion on this point by itself. To me, as a believer of God, this is when it gets embarrassing. I actually don't know whether to give all blame to these fallen leaders for how they let everyone down that had expectations of them or whether to give fault to those that put so much confidence in man. We should understand that one of the primary reasons for Jesus Christ coming to earth was to prove that He could overcome all earthly temptation, because no man was capable of possessing this ability to resist temptation but Him.

Religion and its leaders might reconsider its methods used in the past concerning its intolerance for homosexuality. In doing so, it does not need to change any of its basic beliefs; it needs only to live by the message that it teaches others—which is to love your neighbor as you love yourself, or judge ye not yet ye be judged—and to leave the rest of it to God. To most believers, homosexuality is a lifestyle choice. This lifestyle is viewed by religious leaders and most followers of God as a sinful way to live our lives.

This brings me to an important question: if everyone wore a label displaying their lifestyles, how would homosexuality blend in with everyone else? Just imagine if everyone's labels were attached to all different believers of religion while they are revealing all their dark secrets of life to everyone who sees us. If this were possible, I'm sure all sorts of things would be exposed. If everyone did this, some labels of ours would read, "I'm a rapist" or "I love pornography" or "I used to be a heroin addict." The point that I'm trying to make is, if we decide to unveil our dark secrets by putting it on display for the world to see, this world will judge us for what we revealed. I suppose this could be why most of us conceal what we don't want others to know about us. In fact, most religious people will not want their dark secrets exposed, even if they feel that it's okay to live that way privately. Most of us won't fully claim this. Often, because of who we are, we become overconfident in our thinking that God's favor will be upon us. So between our wrongdoing and our prayers, most feel their business is done. But in reality, a majority of people are themselves wrestling, struggling, and attempting to better understand God, even those with high and powerful positions in our religious institutions.

It's important to realize that until recent history, thousands of years of our evolution in religion have evolved with homosexuality in different ways which are no different than other things such as: witchcraft, leprosy, adultery, blasphemy, etc. These other things were also dealt with by those of religious faith just as severely, if not worse, than people do now with homosexuality. Religion does have a bloody history, with past leaders defending the traditions of their religious beliefs. That history should be an example of how our religious persecution can actually have the opposite intended effect of trying to change those we've condemned and persecuted. It's important for us to understand that religion was designed to promote love of all life and that its purpose was to encourage others to believe in a God of love. However, today, it's possible that just trying to explain this belief with others can actually promote hate. Even today, some will kill people over their different religious beliefs or traditions. What I don't understand is why our religious beliefs are often the driver of our desires to judge and persecute others.

If we really examine religion as well as its followers and members, you will find the examples of this world: some good, some bad, some stupid, and most lost and searching to find themselves as it relates to our Creator and his laws for mankind. The intolerance for homosexuality in our religions might change when those who follow it can clearly understand how to worship with homosexuals without feeling as though it is not at the expense of their spiritual walk with God. In fact, we should be teaching believers of our religion that it is a blessing from the Creator of life that comes our way when we extend love to those that we otherwise would not consider. Nevertheless, those that disagree with this concept of thinking must first consider that God's desires for every one of us is to love as an example before condemning others.

Since mankind's beginning, religion and homosexuality have been an oil-and-water type of mixture, and it still remains that way to this day. The hope is that the institutions of God will eventually find a way to better support homosexuals' request for this kind of acceptance with their members. For this to happen, those doing this must be certain and comfortable of the facts and how they affect our religious beliefs. They must also understand why it prevents homosexuals from having religious equality. They should have the belief that confirms what God requires of us, which is to love thy neighbor. In the past, other methods that have been used to influence homosexual tolerance were radically different and were not effective in creating harmony in religion with homosexuality. The religious leaders and believers have not been able to embrace any new concept or approach for communicating with homosexuals. Instead, we are more comfortable to pass judgment on those that don't meet our criteria, and sometimes on the most basic of issues.

Another one of the objectives of this book is to encourage those with different religious beliefs to educate their followers as to how they can live by the fundamentals of their religion without condemning others for the way they live. I'm confident that after doing this, we will lead our lives with a deeper consideration for our level of compassion that we have for others, even if it hurts us. We begin to love those we don't like. Eventually, we must believe that we reap benefit from our actions, especially when we represent a religion of love. We begin to lead our lives by the method of love. Ultimately, we learn that this is the best way to promote change in any situation, especially to those that we have differences with. The question could then be: Does religion and its leaders and followers have the authority to judge, or is that not until judgment day for the Almighty to decide? I would argue that because of man's nature, unless we all keep our affairs to the world private, that it inevitably may lead to condemnation with us—if not. Religion has long opposed anyone who operates outside their traditions, and those that don't live by these standards are usually held to the very same considerations. This influences many people in purposely not revealing personal things to others in fear of what some may think and say. This popular response by most people is from a fear of becoming a victim or a target of religious persecution because of others knowing about their personal affairs.

The intolerance that some religious people have for homosexuality is not the fault of our institutions, as it may be more of a reflection of just how we have become desensitized to how others feel. Moreover, it reflects how we have become ineffective in teaching the biblical laws that require us to have tolerance for homosexuals so that the followers in our religion understand. It seems that our teachings do not help teach religious people how to accept those who are homosexuals while also living by our religious traditions and beliefs. The recent fall of different religious leaders has helped damage religion's influence on those that would otherwise believe. In today's ever-evolving society, our leaders of religion has somehow failed to come up with creative ways of finding its voice to teach others. This does not indicate that those that represent religion do not understand how to love people that are not like themselves. It's more that religion has not allowed itself to be redefined. What has hindered this change partially is because of the leaders and their wrongdoings, and this has negatively impacted those that view religion. Many religious institutions today are trying to do just that—rebuilding trust in those that have already witnessed its failures. This is perhaps proving to be more difficult than some might have thought. Nevertheless, the lesson that should be learned is that any time mankind is in control of anything, we are capable of being wrong. Also, we must not necessarily look at others as our example of religion to follow, unless we consider the significant potential of those that we follow could be leading us the wrong way. In other words, the concept of religion, as perfect as it may be sometimes, is only as effective as its leaders.

We all must understand that those that teach anything at all about religion do so from their learned perspective based on their own past experiences. Everyone's walk with God is different. Those that represent the leadership of religion are just as human as all of us, and they are capable of being wrong as well. In fact, they're exposed to more temptation than most others to do wrong. One of the many problems with our thinking is that we all struggle with emotions that are influenced by things around us. We feel differently toward different people, depending on a wide range of complex reasons that demonstrate how it is that all people are not alike and are unique in the way we all processes information differently. However, when seeking a religion, we all seek the same results and that is a spiritual relationship with God that gives purpose in our life and death. We are all imperfect and are all capable of being wrong in our thinking, but we are all students of religion and life, and if we have concluded that there is nothing more to learn and that we know all there is to know about religion and have chosen to be a teacher instead, then we have limited our ability to continue learning, and we no longer will have the opportunity to mature as we should. We must understand that none of us own religion, and neither does anyone have the right to enforce penalty of judgment for God's law. Even God instructs us in the Scripture that vengeance is his alone.

Most of today's religious believers attempt to live life as an example and as proof to others of what they believe in their religion. While doing this, our failures are actually sometimes considered by some to be an example of man's inability to live by what he or she teaches others. In fact, it's an example of how mankind has failed religion and God. If we show kindness to those that are unpleasant to us, this would be the perfect example and the real concept of what our religion actually teaches us. I believe this is one of the examples of how God intended for us to live as well.

The popular biblical quote that tells one to "turn the other cheek" if one is struck on their cheeks by someone is a good example of my point. In fact, turning one's cheek after being struck is not a cowardly act, but rather a point that God attempts to make to everyone—especially those in religion to be nonaggressive in their attempt to influence the change in others through love, patience, and long-suffering. You must admit that these are not the personal traits of most people, religious or not.

Nonetheless, the point is that religion is sometimes only effective as those that lead it. Giving liberty to this thought allows those with preconceived negative feelings about religious people to now separate man from the institution of religion. This will allow others to understand better that we all represent religion, whether we believe it or not, and that there is a part that God has considered about all of us and understand how we are all part of his plan. Also, in his written Word, warning was given to those who read the Bible that there will be many leaders who will falsely represent his Word in an attempt to disrupt the Lord's plans for those He has created. This is better witnessed especially when religious messages of love are now interpreted by some to be the example of the Almighty's unjust judgment on the world for what he hates of us, when in reality the primary thing He hates are those things which are the opposite of love. We must not rely on others for our facts about God. It should be for every individual to seek and find on their own.

It's important for us to realize that these Bible scriptures and most biblical text that were written before Jesus's birth and are still taught today are the thoughts and beliefs of others from the past that have recorded their knowledge of things learned in their lifetime from their experiences. Everyone must now establish their very own relationship with our Creator and must independently be certain about biblical facts as they did. Again, we are all no more important to God from one to another in our attempt to gain access to him directly. Let no man fool you that his or her walk with religion is more important than yours. The Bible states that on the day of judgment, there will be many ministers that will be astonished when they learn that God will not recognize them as eligible for his kingdom in Heaven.

One of the basic points that I make in this chapter is to suggest that my readers should search independently for the understanding of religion and consider that when man attempts to follow its interpretation of the Bible instead of what God intended for us, it further highlights our failure to be reliable in leading others. God and religion will always remain, but mankind has proven that his or her relentless quest to conform and adapt to it will always be questionable, making the responsibility of those that attempt to follow religion to do so with humbleness and great caution.

One of the things that most of us would agree on is that we would not want to be falsely accused or stereotyped by anyone especially through hearsay. I believe that our God is the same. He wants us all to know him first before we judge him. Why should we expect all others to live by that standard if we are not willing to give our Creator the same respect? Most of us do not like it when someone improperly rephrases or changes what we meant or misrepresents our views about something. Our Creator actually feels and thinks the way we do. With this subject, I illustrate how God is perfect even when He created man. It also shows how He is not untouched by mankind's ungodly acts as well, even when it's being done by those He has created. However, this should serve as our example of why it is up to every individual to seek religion for their own understanding based on facts that come from their learned experience. We must not be persuaded by others and their opinion of Scriptures or their interpretation of God's laws to be considered by us as fact. Jesus Christ being crucified on the cross is the proof of the mistakes that man has already made in the name of religion, and it further demonstrates how God himself is not immune from the hatred of mankind. I believe that those that wanted Christ persecuted did so with the thinking that they had just cause. They probably felt it was not only the right thing to do but that it was also in defense of their belief and their traditions.

I often wonder what the motives were of those who wanted Jesus executed, and if they were influenced by the pressure from their religious leaders and others in the mob that wanted him killed. From this, it seems we learn that most of us are likely to bear judgment on others even today, without us reflecting on ourselves and our mistakes.

The religion's inability to stop itself from the condemnations of others in the past strengthens my belief today that religious leaders and believers are no different than from the day and times when Jesus Christ was judged and executed. In fact, some of them participated in the persecution of Christ. If we could imagine being in that day and time of Jesus's execution, we would have the chance to witness the mobs of people demanding for His death. But an ancient king called Herod might have done differently. He was ultimately influenced by many angry people in the mob that wanted him to condemn Christ. Those that had formed their opinions did so without giving Jesus a fair court hearing or hearing the evidence for His defense, but they did not. What is also so disturbing is that most of those that wanted his death had no problem doing so without having any proof. Today, our society is similar in thinking to those who were involved in His crucifixion. We condemn others without being fully aware of the facts. Sometimes, it seems that we do this as if it is a duty to this world and to God, as they did with Christ.

Most of us who believe in religion and God attempt to judge others on the basis of our tradition and belief. I think that most may do this with good intentions. What's interesting is that in the days that He was crucified, those who judged Jesus really never met him. They most likely only heard about the Lord from His ever-increasing popularity. This is where the problem begins with most of us—when we hear gossip about someone.

In the case of Jesus Christ, His problem also began because He had conducted miracle healings of many sick people and brought back to life those who had died. When Jesus helped people, some would claim that He was doing so with witchcraft or that He blasphemed against God when He claimed to be the son of God. For us today, this should serve as proof of what mankind may do or how this can happen to anyone if it can happen to Jesus

Himself. It further demonstrates how we can be wrong in our perception of others and how things could differ if we don't fully investigate first before we make judgments on others. When everyone agrees on the same idea of almost anything, it can give us more reason to believe that we're more connected with the truth. When we're in a situation in which everyone agrees with our views, we can become blinded from seeing other alternatives. We are not able to independently view things differently without being influenced by what others think. When we are hearing and believing other's opinions instead of facts, then people's opinions become just like facts to us.

For me, the solution to this problem was simple: Don't trust the opinions of others and investigate things yourself. You should always be led by your educated decision and not by what others may say.

History has proven that religious persecution is always led by the few who have established and enforced these traditions for believers. As a society, we are all followers of something. Our religious beliefs are not established because of what we've created in religion, but rather, they are a reflection of our choice in which version of religion we've chosen to believe. I feel that is where the diversity of religion becomes confusing. The traditions of other religions can be so different, and at times it appears that we all see things differently. What we learn we share with others, and most of us expect others or those we've told to adapt or convert to our way of thinking about religion.

It seems that we are all followers of our religion. How can we be considered leaders if religion was not discovered by us? We are not the one who has personally witnessed all the recorded biblical events. We are followers because of what we believe was not personally witnessed by us. Giving deep thought to this fact leads me to understand better that if we did not create religion, how can we regulate or enforce it? Is that not for who created it?

Also, how do we know who the Creator is if we have not met the Creator personally?

If we understand God only through the eyes and the experiences of others, then we must question ourselves as to whether our belief in our religion is established by others or if it comes about because of our personal efforts to actually seek to find the facts about what we believe about God and religion. I suppose I really want everyone to question themselves on this issue. Do we lead or follow in our religious belief, especially if it relates to our opinions of people that do not meet our standards? A belief that we follow sometimes without facts even when we have found religion, and after we understand, it seems that it can still be difficult to get everyone to follow the laws of it despite this.

Our religious leaders of past and present are a direct example of this. Their attempt to follow their teachings and beliefs can often be compromised by having self-righteousness as a result of being in such a position. Eventually some think that because they are a religious leader, that they are favorable to God. It is a struggle for most of them to comprehend just how insignificant to the Almighty they can become by having pride in themselves. I believe all of us have at some point in the past have had a chance at the management of someone's life, whether it was our loved one or a job. However, most would agree that it potentially can feel empowering to those who have never led before. Even those who have led others for a great part of their career have most likely determined that this authority can be misused and presents a temptation for those to feel superior to others.

Understanding that this great pressure of temptation for those of religious authority exists has helped me understand the true reality of our leaders, and it highlights their human flaws. This is the point that we must understand: that religious people are not different from all others. They are not necessarily our examples of what we should always follow. What is often misunderstood about our religious leaders is when they do lead us, how exactly should we follow? What can be gained by understanding more about them, and how could finding out the answer be helpful in getting us closer to our knowledge of religion and God? For some, knowing that there are others who have faults and whose struggle on earth with religion is no different than theirs helps them to relate better to religion as they are able to witness the experience of others just like them that are spiritually struggling to understand who God is. That's essentially why it's not a good idea to use our leaders as examples in life for us to follow. Rather, they should be seen as more of examples of someone who has volunteered to put themselves in such a controversial position. Usually, our ministers have done this as an act of their belief, and they endure more temptation to do wrong than the average believer or unbeliever. What they experienced can be used as a tool for all of us as we navigate our relationships with God, using how they have lived as our example of what to do as well as what not to do.

It is important for us to understand that there are other essential things about religion and its traditions that shapes and forms the basis for our opinions. It begins with what we are expecting from religion itself. I mean, let's face the facts and realities about this subject. We all have an opinion about how religious leaders and believers should be or how we would expect them to treat us. Our opinion throughout our lifetimes have probably changed or evolved to other levels of thinking. What motivates most of us to be connected to religion is that we're usually expecting results from something. Because of our relationship with God, we usually expect Him to protect us either in our earthly journey or in our spiritual life after death, or both

If God or religion had nothing to offer that most of us could measure or believe, then most of us would not be interested in investing our energy and time with religion or God. Factually, we must have a desire or a need that motivates all of us either way about knowing or not wanting to know about God or religion.

Essentially, we must answer the question about what we are seeking from God and religion. In other words, what do we expect from God when we're seeking Him, and if we're disappointed in God, why is that so? This method of thinking promotes those that do to begin to seek understanding about religion and God more independently than before. Also, it helps to understand that all those who believe in God are no closer to Him than any of us, because it is written that He is not a respecter of persons. We all share the responsibility to know His written laws by searching, just as those in the Bible did. If we hold ourselves as accountable as we hold other people, we might find things we don't like about ourselves, as we do with others.

Sometimes, we robotically conduct our daily lives, and as a consequence of doing this, we do not grow in understanding. Also, we are being disingenuous in our attempt to live a religious life or in our attempt to really understand our religion. Essentially, we all want to feel more connected to our Creator, and most of us think that religion is our main way to find that connection. However there are those who believe that religion becomes a great burden to its followers because of its many religious conditions. This should be when our independent thinking should kick in and make us want to independently investigate the facts about what we believe.

We begin to understand that no one has this exclusive right to religion over anyone else who is truly seeking it. It is written that God is knocking on the door of all our hearts and that if anyone will open up their hearts to Him, he will come in and sup with us. This access to the Lord is available for everyone who seeks love. God is love, and he can be found through anyone's desiring heart that seeks him. I suppose because of this lack of anyone mentioning this fact as being a necessary thing for us to learn about our religious leaders and their human flaws. It has influenced some people to treat certain leaders as their god. Their enormous persuasion of their leadership over others can be a strong influence, persuading some to love them and to think of our leaders as inhuman and with no flaws. I believe that this fact has been overlooked as it relates to when we are following the traditions of our religion. This can be used as our example of how good and bad traditions can originate.

As mankind attempts to better understand the logic of our religion, we also begin to understand how the Almighty can love those that we don't love. This is when we begin to arrive at this new reality that we are not the only ones important to God. We need to give room for Him to love others as He said and with faith try to use this as our example for what we believe and teach to others. It is our responsibility for us to not only get to know who the Almighty is but also to understand that everyone has their own different path that gets them there to that reality, whether it is our leaders or followers of religion. If possible, both could use the faults of others as their justification for their lack of belief in religion. This does not help us in our personal quest to know God; rather, it shows that we all have a need to be loved by our Father in heaven and that despite this, no one is more privileged than another in His eyes.

I think that sometimes our religious leaders and believers act as if religion is only for them, and some actually feel that others that don't believe as they do are people who are outside looking in. Only fools behave this way, and they are considered foolish because they do not consider that God's directive is for us to share the message about His love with others that don't know him. Sometimes, what our leaders confess to believe may conflict with how some really feel within themselves. Often, they can act as if they are privileged instead of being privileged to help others. However, what they do is no different than the average person who has a new designated authority over others. Anyone having authority over peoples' lives, if not careful, can feel some sense of self-pride, and with this prestige, we feel that we have become privileged. It's hard to ignore when we are doing financially or socially better than others or when others' standards of the way they live are substandard in our views. It's really difficult for us to ignore these facts, and it can be deceiving when we begin to feel that we are superior over others, as we also begin to feel less superior to those that are doing better than we are.

Sometimes, holding firm to our religious values is not as simple as we think. I feel that essentially we are all guilty of not admitting these facts, and this is also demonstrated when anyone can truly feel that they are on the same human level as those that have much less than they do. Expecting change to those in the religious world or its institutions may only be possible with time. It is logical that God would want fairness and order in all things that we do. We know that with time, all things are usually capable of change; but what we generally don't calculate is that with time, God can change all of us and that all of us are capable of being reshaped. I suppose the point I'm trying to make is that religion and its leaders and believers should be given the same chance as everyone else.

History has proven that over time, as a society, we do evolve. The hope is that we are evolving in the right way of what our Creator has intended for us and in the way our society and world needs. It's obvious that if we are led by man, it will always result in the kind of confusion that we are experiencing today. Again, religion will always exist, but the only things that most likely will change is mankind, the traditions that we live by, and the way we perceive others as it relates to our religion and our traditions from it. Essentially, change happens *within us* first, and if we are persistent, it will ultimately become more in line with what God intended for us. History has proven that religious leaders have been wrong before in their persecutions of others, making the point that those who seek religion or God must have a sincere desire to follow.

With each passing of each generation, the result of different ways history has impacted religion can be better seen and learned from. Also, in each new generation, it becomes more noticeable how our religious traditions are slowly changing and evolving. Nevertheless, we as individuals collectively inspire this change in the traditions of our future. Sometimes, as we set out to change God and religion, many times we are changed by God ourselves in this process. Oftentimes, things we did not know before can later be revealed by the process of us doing this. But without us attempting to seek God, we often don't find him.

If we all understand that religion is still evolving and that we are part of that evolution, we would better understand just how we all are connected by our Creator. Understanding that God created religion and man created most traditions should help us to know that we cannot blame God for things mandated by mankind. We can only find fault in the traditions of men whose persecution of others were not intended by God.

In the written words of the Almighty, it's clear that His first desire is to ultimately be with all of us. What is unclear is who will qualify. When we die, it will only be a two-way dialogue with us and our Creator. There will be no need for religion or its leaders at this point. Our earthly communication should be the same way. We are required to deal directly with Him. No man or religion can do that for us. Religion is just a way mankind worships and serves Him, demonstrating their belief while on Earth through their traditions. But death is when we all have to get real about everything. No one is there but you and the Lord.

In general, our approach to religion and those that follow their belief about religion have similarities. All of us do so in the same way; our search is similar. We all are imperfect when we attempt to live by our religious traditions as examples to others. If we begin to understand that it is our responsibility to meet the Lord now and not later and if we do wait until later, we cannot blame the Almighty Himself for what we don't know about Him. I believe that we all are responsible to know who we serve and the definition of what religion is. Everyone will personally deal with God after death and without anyone to represent us, except Jesus Christ. I feel that this is the central point in understanding religion. We all are on an equal playing field when it comes to getting access to our heavenly Father and getting the opportunity of understanding religion. Our journey begins and is activated when we seek Him.

Everyone's access to our heavenly Father does not come from religion or religious leaders. It begins with our desire to sincerely know God and demonstrate love for others. It still remains our responsibility to seek the truth about religion. We should realize that when we die, what happens between God and us will only matter when we go to settle the score, and then we shall know at that time the many mysteries that were never possible in our new relationship with our Creator.

2

Discovering That Someone Straight
Is Now Gay

So this is the big moment. Now is when everything really goes down. It is the time when you discover that the person you have known possibly all your life now has another identity. Moments like this have been shared by many friends and family alike around the world, all ending in very different results. With me, I felt I had to adapt to the situation, and how I did this was something I decided to share with others. With me, the ones that were gay were special because they were my two sisters. Don't get me wrong. I was guilty of condemning them at first with my judgment, but I backed off. The fact is that I wasn't prepared for this battle mentally or emotionally at that time. I began to realize, after finding out that they were gay, that what I do now will later define who I've become as a big brother to them. I immediately reflected on all other homosexual situations that I could remember to help me prepare for this. I was attempting to find a solution for them. At that time, it seemed to me that they must not have been thinking so clearly or that something in their lives was bothering them and was causing their homosexuality. It was very confusing for me.

It wasn't as if the notice of one's sexuality change comes with an instruction manual that shows everyone how to properly act or think. I felt that if this had been anyone else other than my sisters, it would've been different. I'm certain that I would not have had concern for others as I did for them. I became speechless with others about this topic. I kept asking myself, "How do you fix something like this?" It literally took weeks of not saying much to others as I spent most of my time busy in thought. Many times this was a result of an emotional black cloud that I felt was over me. I couldn't help but feel that somehow, something that was once so close to me now seemed so far away. I thought of many different scenarios of how my sisters have become this way and who might be influencing them. Then there was this awful feeling that I had deep down inside of me—that as a man, maybe something was undesirable about us that I didn't fully understand. I wondered what these types of women thought about men. Were they afraid of us? Some of them looked at me as if I didn't exist when trying to speak to them. I assumed that maybe they thought that I was flirting with them. Despite this, I thought that they often acted as if all men were infected.

I come from a large family with eight siblings. One of my sisters often acted as a *tomboy*, which is the term we used back then for girls that played with boys or liked toys for boys instead of dolls. Nevertheless, I never thought of her being a tomboy as being abnormal. On Sundays, my mom usually dressed my sisters up for church in very elaborate dresses, especially on Easter Sunday or special holidays. It sometimes seemed as a competition in church with all the other pretty dresses that other girls wore. Seeing my sisters dressed this way painted a very different picture of who they might be in their future. I thought that they were very beautiful in the way they carried their baskets on Easter Sunday. What they wore had large petticoat slips underneath that elevated their dresses outward. It was a magical moment in my young life, seeing them dressed that way, especially with their matching socks, shiny shoes, and pretty bows tied in their hair. As a brother, I did not realize until later in my life that I had grown so sensitive over little stuff like this with my sisters. These things are part of what made me feel that they would marry a man one day and have a family from that relationship. *These are the memories that those who were new in her life were not there to know or remember as I did,* I thought. That was an important point to me—that her friends now weren't there to experience those previous memories of the past between my sisters and me. It seemed to me that I should have the privilege in their lives over their friends.

As selfish as it sounds, I feel that this really does reflect how most of us think when we're faced with a discovery that someone we love is gay. I really felt that I deserved an explanation from them. Actually, I wanted to have a verbal confrontation with them and win, which I felt I would then have had the influence to change them. While that is probably more accurate of how I felt—believe me though—I never had enough courage to say it until now. I don't know if this was good or not—that is, not expressing to others how we actually think. I'm certain that it probably would have destroyed my relationship at that time if I had tried. The fact is that it would not have changed them anyway, and I would have lost more than I would have gained after telling them how I thought. I felt all of this was not worth risking.

As I was attempting to rationalize and justify the way I felt about them being gay, I found it hard to get into a confrontation with my sisters about their homosexuality. But just in the event that it happened, I tried to save the strongest and most compelling reasons to justify my feelings for last, such as religion. I felt that I needed to share my feeling with them of how I felt that homosexuality was a wrong thing for them. One of the expectations that my one sister did make clear to me was that she wanted me to respect that this is her "life partner" that she loves and is committed to, despite how I felt. At that time, I did not want to hear my sister defend her position on this issue because I would usually get upset—mainly because I disagreed with them and could not verbalize intelligently my point of views. There was nothing else of substance other than religion as my defense against their life choices.

I suppose that being their brother, I was expecting that my sister's intimate friends would be men and that naturally, they would have more things in common with me than their female relationships—although females presented a different experience that otherwise would not have been possible. Otherwise, before this, I only knew of females that were attracted to men, and my competitions in dating women were always limited to men. Now the thought of a female competing with men for other women was a new and wild thought to consider for me. It seemed as if men have just become insignificant to some women just for being a man and not because of other undesirable qualities that we have. It felt weird to me that the thought of a woman is now our competitor in this scheme of dating women. I really felt that this was insulting and degrading. It wasn't how I felt about them dating other women, but rather how some of them acted uncomfortably around me just because I'm a man. In most cases, they never knew me; they were only introduced to me. I had not formed any opinion about them, but it seemed as if they did about me. It seemed that I really never paid any attention to the fact that my sister's friends and relationship with others were always with other females rather than with men.

I began analyzing past experiences from memory regarding my sisters' homosexuality, and as I began to recall how things were at that time, my emotions about it would change like that of a clock every hour. It seemed that with each hour I was experiencing different feelings and thoughts. The first of what I remember experiencing was being embarrassed, and it was followed immediately by anger at something that I could not directly blame. I had the emotions to cry, but I pushed back from doing so, at least in public. Not discussing this subject with anyone allowed me to pretend as if it really wasn't happening. It became a practice for me to notice homosexuals more than ever before. It became necessary for me to notice how they walked, talked, or dressed. It was difficult for me to stop myself from over analyzing everything. As time evolved, it became common to run into someone who was gay mainly at work and in social events. It was important to me to always project a face that states that I enjoy them and their friends, despite how I felt. To me, it seemed that their smiles and their laughter were sort of seductive. I enjoyed how they could light up a room with their presence. I asked myself, how can these people be so joyful? I had to admit that most homosexual people showed more feelings and compassion for others as if they genuinely cared for them compared to most people that I knew who were religious.

Later, I felt it was necessary for me to understand more clearly how my mom, brothers, and other sisters felt about my sisters' homosexuality, only to realize that it was just as puzzling to other family members as well. Despite my opinion, most of my family were more accepting of this and thought differently than the way I felt. Although I knew and understood all the biblical reasons why we should advocate against homosexuality, the answer always eluded me as to how we could balance that with love. What was puzzling to me was how can you be against something, yet be *for* the very something that you're against in the beginning? As confusing as that sounds, I believe everything was more confusing for me at that time about homosexuality.

Nevertheless, I felt as though what I was doing could be considered by some as being nosey about my sisters, and it made me wonder how my sisters would react if they found out that I was uncomfortable and confused about them. My youngest sister was more well-known in our church than I was. She sang in the church choir, which traveled around the nation. At that time, I was actually inspired by her commitment to religion and her family. I always felt that this church served as a second home to me and my family. However, what I regret is that after having known most members there for years and because of my sister's homosexuality, I had shut down from communicating with many members of our church as well as with family and friends. I thought and hoped that this was possibly just a phase that my sisters were experiencing and that I would damage their reputations if I continued talking about it with everyone. The fact of my potentially having to face most people we knew and having to reveal details about my sisters' homosexuality—not knowing how different people would react or what they would say—was what I feared. I even felt the same way with our relatives, such as my cousins, aunts, uncles, etc. Yet I think that for others and their families, most tend to continue to ignore what is happening by not engaging with their family in any conversation about one's sexuality. It seems as if we learn to pretend just enough to keep relationships nurtured, so we don't lose the close connections with those that we care about.

After my parents' divorce, it seemed as if my mom struggled privately and inwardly. She tolerated this new experience of my sisters' homosexuality unlike everyone else in our family. I became amazed and shocked, totally not knowing what to expect next. There was a deep and awful inward feeling of shame I felt that was puzzling to me, especially being as though I wasn't the one doing this. I felt this way probably because my sisters were very close to me, and I also felt that it was against our religious traditions. It seemed strange that the act of remembering the feeling of this experience is what makes it more difficult to explain my reasons for reacting this way. Although it was not something I would dare say out loud, it only became something that I would think about privately every now and then. I was afraid of sharing this with someone as I wasn't exactly sure how they would respond.

I think the pressure of potentially having a conversation about homosexuality with my sisters was a very scary thought for me, and it was one of the reasons why I avoided discussing the subject with anyone as well. I later felt that maybe I should have talked to them about my feelings in the beginning instead of letting so many years go by. However, the conversation that I would have had back then with my unevolved thinking would have made things worse in my relationship with them. If I had done this, they would have felt as if I was telling them what they should do or not do with their life, and that by itself would have been the wrong approach. Eventually, one of my sister's attitudes became that of a rebel with a cause, knowing exactly what she wanted and being very clear to everyone not to stop her or get in the way. At that time, both of their homosexuality went unchallenged by any of our family. We all were raised with parents that had deep religious convictions about homosexuality, yet no one in our family that I knew of ever discussed this or any other similar subject with my sisters in a confrontational way.

Looking back at all of this, it seemed strange that no one in my family felt a need to preach or condemn my sisters for what they were doing. It felt like the zombie effect had taken place in all of us. Everyone seemed unspoken about their religious beliefs contradicting with our sisters being homosexual. It appeared as if we were sleepwalking or in another dimension or something. I never asked anyone in my family what they thought or how they felt, and no one ever asked me as well. However, it was clear to me that everyone should have some sort of opinion, yet no one would voluntarily talk about it. Perhaps I must have been affected by this zombie-like effect as well.

My wife was the one who revealed to me that my one sister was homosexual. This became obvious to her before I was aware of it. This all began after I had discovered love letters from her friend that was in my sister's car seat. As I read her letters, I became confused about what I was reading, and that is when my wife told me that my sister was a homosexual and that she had a relationship with someone. Later, I regretted having cursed at my wife out of my anger, blaming her of false accusations about my sister. I did not understand why I was so angry at my wife for saying this. Later, the reality came to me that we were now one of the families that had homosexuality in them. I was fully aware that there were people who would really condemn those who were gay as well as their families, and I feared that it would happen to us. I once felt that our family was always an example of how a family should be, and now because of that, I was no longer able to claim this.

Years later, we realized that my niece and her daughter were also gay. I knew of my niece's homosexuality and always suspected that she and all of her friends might influence her daughter. I'm not suggesting that this is why my niece's daughter is that way; I'm only telling you what I felt before it happened as a matter of truth. However, when I would visit with my eldest sister and her family, my niece and her daughter were usually there. I thought as a great-uncle that I had a responsibility to be a good example to her, showing her things that maybe she lacked from not having a father and having only the experience of a mother who was homosexual. At the very least, I wanted her to have an opportunity to be influenced by a male figure. I wanted to have an uncle relationship with her.

It seemed as if I was repeating what I had done years ago with my sisters. I suddenly realized that I have now experienced three generations of my family that turned out to be gay. Unlike before, I did not blame myself or condemn anyone for how they lived. I no longer had a desire to confront them with my God or claim that they were not going to heaven because of how they lived. I assumed that most likely, they had already been told this by others, and they had already made a choice of how they want to live. It started to feel that my attempt to force-feed them a message about God's judgment of how they should live would have no effect other than creating animosity between us. Because of this, I made the choice for the first time that I would rather live as the example of what I want those that I love to know. I think my example of how I did continue to hang in there with them and share their life's journey with them is more persuasive, and to me, it feels like more of what was the right thing to do. It almost eliminates the terrible feelings that everyone gets from being angry at each other, which has proven to be a waste of energy for us.

One of my brothers was more firm in his religious beliefs against homosexuality. In the beginning, he showed very little respect to those that presented their support of homosexuality equality to him. His justification was that he stood on the foundation of biblical scriptures. My other brothers were much more liberal. My other two brothers later shared their views of accepting the homosexuality of my sisters and others. It was not because they necessarily agreed with this as a way to live but more because they chose not to judge or really speak any negative opinion about it. The fact that all of my older brothers were not firmly against this really did confuse me. I don't know why I expected them to be as mad as I was and why I was disappointed when they did not get angry. I suppose my goals were to change my two sisters or find support from my brothers to help change them by trying to get them to be passionate about it as I was. Although my mom did not verbalize her feelings to me, she successfully struggled with its conflict with her belief, although she finally found peace through her love and tolerance despite her Christian beliefs.

However, my other sisters responded with a totally different approach compared to my brothers. One of my two straight sisters never spoke anything negative about homosexuality. Although one sister did seem critical in private of their homosexual affairs, she still pretended to embrace everyone as friends despite who they were. My other straight sister seemed halfway curious about it all. I believe she might have had some personal experience with this in the past, but she ultimately stayed straight. Yet she remained as a noncritical friend to homosexuals that she met. I believe she struggled eternally with this temptation to be with other women, but I'm not sure what ultimately played a part in her decision to stay straight.

For me, the discovery of my two sisters to be gay was something I never wanted to talk about as a topic of my conversation with anyone for several years. I guess part of me did not want to admit that maybe I was wrong for feeling so angry about their conversion. I began to notice that the closeness that we once shared was changing. How it was changing, I wasn't exactly sure. I thought that maybe my inner feelings about how I really felt were perhaps more revealing to them than I thought. If not, could it be that this newfound relationship that she has discovered has now become more important than the relationship we shared before?

It was different with my eldest homosexual sister. After many years later, our relationship grew very close; with the youngest one, we've become very distant from each other. This of course happened over time, although I was never able to figure out exactly why our relationship grew distant. My suspicion was that it was because of my disappointment of her and that I've always told her how proud I was of her before I knew she was gay. Formerly, she then sang in a choir in church on most Sundays before my mom passed away. After my mom's death, she suddenly changed her religion and her sexuality. Hereafter was when I discovered her homosexuality. This was totally different when compared to the eldest of the two; with my youngest sister, it was so unexpected given the way she was before. She was married, had kids, and was intensely attending church. So between the two ways of learning that both were gay, this for some reason was more difficult to accept. I began to think that I had became insignificant to her because of what my religious beliefs are and how it judges homosexuality, but having the realization that she once believed in these same values was confusing to me. I suppose we are all capable of change in our lives, but to accept the sudden change of ones sexuality and their religion is not so simple for someone like me to accept or understand, and I'm certain it is the same way for many others.

I'm sure there has to be great pressure on homosexuals when they reveal themselves to those that never knew that they were gay, but it is as intensely difficult for others to digest this type of change right away. Everyone is different. I find that some can adapt right away while others can take years to accept, if at all; but certainly, there was pressure for me. Actually, things became confusing at times because I did not know how I truly felt. The mixed emotions I felt of love and hate because of my religious belief and my love for them sort of battled with each other. It's a feeling as if you lost the person that you once knew when you find out something like this. After finding out that someone is gay, we then suddenly realize that we must get to know this person all over again. I believe getting to know someone again is what's relevant to how we feel about the change in others, and also not being able to be certain of things about someone we have known to be a particular way for so long, as the reason why it may create insecurity within our relationship. It has changed the pattern of what we're comfortable with as it relates to our relationship with others. As you may already know, we are not creatures of change.

However, homosexuals and their attempt to share their beliefs with others are very complex. Everyone is so unique and sensitive, and we all have a need to be accepted for our choices in life. This is where most communications breakdowns occur—in the acceptance of someone's homosexuality. People are offended very easily, and we all will defend our values, whether we fully understand them or not. These misunderstandings of our values are shared by both straight people and homosexuals. Most of all these believed values helps to persuade those that have this to possess a degree of belief and pride in what they do believe, and doing this sometimes puts us in an unavoidable conflict with views of others.

In today's society, it does not matter what we actually do or don't believe. We will still be judged by someone about something; if we became a part of anything, it will eventually put us at conflict with something, making it more likely for us to make choices that conflict with others. This could also be the cause of why these divisions between us continue to exist. Our past presents evidence that as a society, we have always condemned others for their different religious beliefs or values. As a society, the challenge now is finding a better way to coexist with our different values or religious beliefs. It's obvious that our need to condemn is triggered by how we feel for others and their lifestyles that don't meet our expectations, whether it is homosexuality or something else.

The fact is that in most cases, most of those who loved another person before they were found to be gay, will most likely always still love them after they find out. It probably doesn't appear that way when most discover this, as they are prone to react with their emotional anger and pain. Many of us will struggle to accept this kind of news. However, the majority of us will become tolerant of gays because our love is ultimately more powerful and persuasive than our hatred or judgment about others. The question then becomes, is it wrong for someone *not to* accept someone's change of their sexuality? I mean, just be honest. If we have people close to us thinking one way and loving them for whom they are, and then that person suddenly changes, I feel it would not be fair to others that are used to the old you. The question could be, why should anyone expect everyone to accept their change? Why not leave open the possibility that we all share responsibility in keeping our relationships healthy with those whom we love and care for? We all have a right to have an opinion. However, despite this, we should be aware and still respect everyone's right to have their opinion in order to live in harmony. I really think this is a major problem for most of us, whether we are straight or gay.

If religious believers cannot fully follow their traditions and beliefs in fear of hurting others that are homosexual and if their teachings have now been considered not socially acceptable, it demonstrates the lack of religious expression and freedom that we now have as a society. It feels as if it's now okay for others to condemn religion and its traditions and also its followers. I suppose the point I'm hoping to make is, just as it is wrong for religion and its followers to make claims that those that are homosexuals are bad people, it is the same issue with those who are homosexuals that condemn traditions of religion and all its followers.

I believe that it's very important that we all recognize how sensitive everyone's emotions are. We should be aware of how we handle our own critiquing of others when dealing in this issue with people. We all have the tendency to accuse others of being the one who initiates the conflict, but I think it takes a lot of effort to suppress how we feel in order to have an open dialogue with those of different views. Often, we feel that when we engage in a verbal conflict with others over our values, we feel that it's necessary to win a dispute in our differences of opinion. Also, we often consider our values and traditions as being more important for others to live by as a condition of our relationship with them, rather than making it a priority in finding a way to find common ground so that a relationship can survive.

I truly believe that we all lose when we fail to keep our relationships healthy after finding that someone is not living the way we expect. We cannot hide the facts from ourselves when we've lost a relationship with someone we care for because of our inability to adapt. As a result, these relationships no longer exist because of how we reacted to someone in accepting or not accepting his or her homosexuality. Usually, we all try to justify our feelings by blaming others and maybe citing the various things that they may have said or done that were wrong. Our refusal to be tolerant of someone who is for or against homosexuality equality can lead to a total breakdown, in what was often a lifetime of a relationship in the making. I feel sad for all those that choose to walk away and turn their heads from the problem. If we are enforcing our belief on others as a condition of having a relationship with them, then this is fundamentally wrong. It doesn't matter if it's our religious views or our views about homosexuality equality or any other views; having conditions of others is what I feel is unfair.

I feel it can be difficult for anyone, straight or homosexual, to navigate their way through all the conflicts that we will be challenged with when trying to accept or trying to convince someone to accept our views. It's our decision to make; either we prioritize our beliefs and traditions as more important or we make our moral values and our consideration for others as being more of a priority. Hopefully, we realize how valuable it is to preserve our relationship with those we care for and love after finding out that they're homosexual. I believe we are capable of possessing enough sensitivity for others, which is necessary for overcoming what will divide our relationships.

We all should recognize that there is a benefit in keeping our relationships healthy with those we normally would not and realize that our failure to do so will forever affect us. If we pretend that our weapons of hate are meant to serve as a point to others, it often will be answered by those we care about with the same response as what we have given to them, thus creating an environment that makes positive change not possible with those we disagree with. It appears at first to be easier to deal with these issues by ignoring or not dealing with what at first seems impossible for us to accept. However, if we don't give up, our possibility for success in our relationships increases.

It's a proven fact that when one chooses to be open about their homosexuality, it affects many people inside and outside of that relationship. Although society today allows for this acceptance to take place more so than times past, this has not broken all barriers that exist. There are those that may love their homosexual relatives but because of their religious traditions or moral values feel that there are no options but to disagree or to disown them. I find it impossible for anyone to get any satisfaction this way. I respect our religious values, but I argue about the methods used by some in dealing with it this way.

I personally would like to feel that my thoughts or decisions regarding someone's choices of life will not only be what God would want, but it also should leave a good feeling within me. I believe that this is the way we should all lead ourselves regarding this and other similar issues of our lives. But as you may know, people will go through extremes in expressing their anger over this kind of topic. Everyone's reason may differ. It doesn't always necessarily mean that religion will be the only motive for such anger. Trying to understand how someone can hate another after finding out that they're a homosexual and how their love can turn to hate is very complex to understand. This logic would lead me to believe that at this point, most of us are so confused that we probably might choose not to exercise our ability to show love. I suppose that we reflect our disappointment and hatred of our loved ones' life choices by treating them similarly to how we ourselves feel within.

When we're thinking that a person is straight and later we find out that they are not, it seems to be an event that's not mentioned as being relevant in relationships in our society. It's not that we don't notice what is happening; it's more that we don't choose to acknowledge the fact that it is affecting us. I believe that most of us pretend to act as if we are not bothered by this, when in fact, most of the time, we are. In our society as secret as kept, most people today are becoming terrified to publicly say what they really feel about homosexuality and when they do express themselves, often it doesn't come out right. I think most of us lack the words to adequately express why we think God is opposed to this without it being more of why we are opposed. In fact, how we were taught to live life while loving all others has created such a conflict within most of us that some of us lack the necessary experience in this area or at least the skill of knowing how to successfully express their point to others about the subject.

In our society, there are those who are *for* homosexuality equality and those that are not, and between these divisions, there really hasn't been a bridge that has brought us together as a society. The extreme differences of opinion between these two beliefs, seems that it will not give in to any agreement. I find that we really don't talk as we should about this subject, and when we do talk, it has an uncomfortable ending. At least for me, it feels as though we are not as open as we could be. We stay guarded about who we are and how we really feel about others. I'm sure we all have had conversations with someone before over homosexuality, and in doing so, it felt as if we had to make up topics to talk about. Sometimes it appears as if there is some sort of disconnect that we have with others about this subject, and I believe that for most of us, we really are afraid to totally say what we feel, whether we are for homosexual equality or not. When we do go there, it's through drinking and being angry or a combination of both. When we really do express how we feel while in this state of mind, we always destroy relationships. The question should be, why should we wait until we are angry or drunk to express how we really feel? Why are we not creative enough to have this conversation now while we are sober and alert? We must be open now to talk to others while we're calm and focused. I'm sure that there are probably other differences we face with others. However, this method should still be applied. We should never approach anything while being angry or intoxicated.

If someone does attempt to fight against homosexuality rights using religion and Scriptures as support, they may need to reconsider the way in which this might be more hurtful than helpful when doing so. As a society, we are so sensitive that even constructive criticism might create a minor war with some people. Nonetheless, finding out that someone we care for is homosexual after not knowing previously can sometimes put us all on the very edge, and it could feel personal to us. We might have always felt like it should be someone else and their family that this only happens to. Some might feel that they now will have to keep this a secret to family or friends. Anyone who thinks and operates this way needs to know that it's perfectly normal to feel this way. What is *not* normal is when we allow our feelings about being *for* or *against* homosexuality to cause us to act violently toward others or to verbally abuse others by condemning their life. I'm even guilty myself of using my God and his Scriptures or hell as my support when I did condemn others for their homosexuality.

From my past, I've learned about most of the slick or sly ways that we justify our actions when we are being unfair to others. Often, our approach in cleaning up the mess we've created ends up being more hurtful than helpful for us and our victims. I've never met anyone that has converted others to religion by way of their condemnation of them; rather, it is usually only through the way they project a true spirit of love for them. As bad as it might hurt us when finding out that someone we care for is homosexual, we must restrain ourselves from saying or doing things that can cause permanent damage to the relationships we value by acting this way. Also, my hope is that those that are homosexual will seek the strength to forgive or overlook people that may have offended them and will allow time for those they cherish to heal and to get balance in their thoughts and emotions as a way to begin to understand those who are against homosexuality.

I would endorse the idea of no one giving up their religion or worship because of being a homosexual but instead to allow God to transform your life to whatever He has for you, just like any other member of religion. The fact that others may see your life choices as not being worthy of it is not the point that should be considered. I believe that the point is in not running away from whatever threatens us but rather facing what bothers us and allowing ourselves to overcome it by dealing with it. I believe that having to live life with this doubt and anger over religion and its followers is worth facing right now while we still are alive. This same message applies to all those in the world. We all need to face God in this life now, instead of waiting until later.

Our walk with the Almighty is a lifetime process, and it is through love that we gain His strength and wisdom. Anyone seeking to deny this relationship with God will also deny themselves the opportunity to learn and grow as needed in their understanding of religion. For anyone to stop seeking God and not worship or not attend church because of what others might say does not give anyone a legitimate excuse. Ultimately, we will all deal with the Almighty one way or another at our death, whether we are for or against homosexuality. The need for our society to get peace about this subject is important. I'm sure that without anyone's direct involvement, society will eventually evolve by itself. However, our concern as a society should be for us to evolve in a way that will secure peace with others as we maintain our values from our religion.

There are generations before us that can be used as our example of how we have evolved from what would be considered extreme barbaric ways of dealing with homosexuality in past societies. At that time, things were so different in our world, and very little was ever discussed about homosexuality. This was considered "in the closet" or "hush-hush," and that was the point. As a society, we have never come together enough to honestly seek solutions for the many different ways that we feel about homosexuality. We're all wounded in some way, and I'm sure we all still recall past hurt and pains. Most times, it may be buried somewhere deep within us. Our religion should not ever be a stumbling block as to why we can't accept those who are for homosexual equality; in fact, our religious beliefs should be the very reason why we are able to. Our religion clarifies our duty to love others, and this is what should drive our Christian desire, which is our need to help others and not our need to judge others. In fact, the Bible has warned us against doing so.

I reflect back on my journey in life as it relates to the homosexuals that are closest to me—that, of course, being my sisters. I recall that whenever I did feel uncomfortable about something, I would usually hide it, and I would try to resolve it within myself what I felt was wrong. I consider this to be an issue that I'm responsible for. I felt that others should not necessarily change how they are; rather, it's up to me to find peace within myself.

Finding that someone we love is homosexual can be overwhelming and devastating to some people. Accepting someone's homosexuality and not wanting to change them is a concept harder than one might imagine. I think that this is the point that maybe we all should consider. Rather than attempt to change others, whether it's getting someone to accept homosexuality or getting someone to change from being a homosexual, maybe it's best that we don't. Everyone's effort to fight for homosexual equality or be against it essentially doesn't really change anyone's views; it only irritates everyone on both sides and widens the gap between finding a peaceful way to live life. Because of this thought and the fact that I don't feel that any one of us will ever be totally satisfied with this world anyway.

I've concluded that I shall accept others for who they are, but most importantly, I shall keep in mind that loving those in this world will always remain a challenge. If my religion is what I believe it to be, then my light shall shine before all men by loving all equally. I hope that everyone has that opportunity to evolve. Our love shall be a guide that helps all of us to accept each other. However, it is a challenge for some of us to accept the life choices of homosexuals, and it's a challenge for homosexuals to find acceptance of our religious society as they advocate for their religious traditions to be recognized against homosexuality. However, our maintaining the fundamental part of who we are is at risk, and that is something we all stand to lose. Essentially, we are all connected socially; we are family. Our social survival is more important than our desire to be treated a certain way. It's our responsibility to know that the choices that we make toward others are just and fair, and we should understand how sensitive some people can be when making these choices. Also, there are so many other issue in this broken world, and they all cannot be solved alone by mankind. But through patience, forgiveness, and the willingness to not give up on those we care about, maybe the hope for a better tomorrow can still exist for all of us within our world and families.

3

How We All Learn to Be Normal Again

This chapter explains my story of what it was like being raised with my two sisters who I thought were straight, and it also describes how my family and I adjusted after finding out about our sisters' homosexuality. It shows the way we found sanity and love for each other in our journey. Though all of our families may deal with challenges that can divide us, there still remain some common things that we all share, and that is that we all want to be loved.

If anyone feels hatred in any way for others regarding homosexuality, this in itself is not a normal thing to feel. Also, when we realize that the challenge given to us in life is learning to live with others that are different from us, we begin to understand how this can hinder or improve our relationships. Also by doing this, we learn that we're able to correspond better with those who have different beliefs that contradict ours. We come to realize that when a family has become divided while in their journey to heal, using these principles as a guide can help us overcome our differences with each other. This should serve as one example of what "being normal again" is.

As you may assume most relationships usually do not overcome from the things that have torn them apart when it comes to our differences over homosexuality with families and friends. I'm sure there could be many different reasons for this that could serve as our foundation and that helps promote our different opinions over homosexuality. Whether it is because of our religious beliefs and traditions or not, the important thing is coming back together and everyone being capable of moving on with their lives without any animosity. Hopefully, this should serve as the example for everyone in knowing what "normal" is. For some, understanding what normal is could be harder than others because of their past experience, which for some might have been extremely more complex compared to others. Sadly, there actually are people who seem to feel absolutely normal when they have animosity with others, as if it is a normal part of life for them. Hopefully, anyone reading this that relates this way would begin to know that there is a genuine joy that we receive when we maintain our relationships, if for no other reason but for our joy.

Our process to heal and adapt to the new changes after learning about someone's homosexuality can be very difficult for some. For others, to just partially heal from it can take years, as it has for me. Over time, our relationships with some people can be tighter than before—that is, if we don't completely give up or destroy what we have left in our relationships. I feel that we all are capable of overcoming our differences in time. However, it's important to not only remind ourselves constantly why we value others but also to be aware of the many different divisions it creates within our families and friends when we fail to find a way to maintain our relationships with those we care about. Sometimes we fail to recognize the point that others indeed add value to our lives through our relationships, whether they are for and against homosexuality. It is not always necessarily about who we are and what we do that should qualify us for this respect, but rather that we all have a story of our experiences of things in our life that others can learn from. The beginning of finding that for me is when I discovered that two of my sisters were gay. There were always certain questions that I had about my sisters' homosexuality, in particular their reasons why they were attracted to women, although this question remained confined in my thoughts.

At that time the acceptance of their homosexuality by our family were limited to our unspoken thoughts which could be witnessed through the expression and tone of everyone in our family. My mom appeared the usual (a face of worldly frustration), moving methodically and fast throughout our home, appearing to not know what tomorrow may bring. I was unsure if as a family our future would be okay. We were a family that was once very well-known and stood as a model for others in our church—that is, before the fall of my dad's ministry. After that occurred, my mom began attending church alone with my sisters. I became worried that things would become much worse for us, mainly because my sisters had changed and our family was divided. At this point, it felt like my mind was in overdrive. I was overanalyzing everything, I thought. I know I must let go, but it really was irritating me daily.

This started my lifelong quest in trying to be "normal again" in the way I viewed my sisters, our family, and also my self-esteem. This led me to discover that it was not just about my sisters but also about my dad's life issues. It was a combination of this and everything else that gave me a feeling of tremendous abnormality in my younger years. It required all of us as a family to redefine ourselves in religion. My mom started working and dating for the first time, which became another event that I felt was responsible for my troubles. I began to think everything that everyone was doing seemed to be wrong—including my mom dating other men after her divorce.

Because of this, I have learned that what we experience in our childhood can be the everlasting example for what we feel is normal or abnormal later on in our lives. Despite what we do in the future, things in our lives will ultimately change as people in our lives will change as well. Therefore, we need to realize that the things that are customary to us one day will change. As a preacher's son and as a developing young man at that time, I tried to feel normal after dealing with the embarrassment of my dad's fallen ministry and also after finding out later that my sisters were homosexual, which both are what contributed to my confusion for many years. It was a double dose of confusion that I felt was responsible for my dilemma at that time. I'm not saying that my dad's actions compare in any way to my sisters homosexuality—no not that at all—but rather that all of these combined experiences are something that are creating this need in me to become "normal again" with my family, my emotions, and my religion.

Some may ask how I can still love my dad after the outrageous and sick things that he had done, and my response would be, "Even though I hate what he has done, I still am able to heal myself when I can forgive him and move on." For me, it's not about me making sure others pay their penalty for their wrong, but rather, it is about trying to overcome what was once bad with what is good. Even though I have every right to hate my dad, I have seen that there is no satisfaction in me having vengeance. I get satisfaction only when I'm able to have forgiveness. When we forgive, we forget our pain, and that is the point. I believe it is too painful for us to deal with others that have hurt us and overcoming this with forgiveness and forgetfulness is therapeutic against those things that hurt us. This method can be used as a way to deal with all our broken relationships and painful experiences in general.

Over time, I began to consider the changes of my family as a very challenging new experience. It was hard adjusting to attending church while we were split up as a family. I never really asked my brothers and sisters how they felt, but for me, life at that time felt so abnormal. Life's changes were not only a struggle for me but for my mom as well. Suddenly, this once first lady of the church was now without a husband, a job, or a day care. The day care part quickly became my responsibility after coming home from high school. Sometimes, my mom worked late nights at a convenient store while I stayed home with my three younger sisters. I felt like an incomplete person without having my dad and other older brothers and sister who had left home already. It seemed to me that it all happened so quickly, though I'm certain now that it was not fast for my mom and sisters.

I later found out that not only had my dad been abusive to my mom, but he had also been accused for many years of sexual abuse by my older sister, who was later raised by my grandmother. I really never realized what he had done until my late adulthood. Yes, I'm talking about my dad who did this to my sisters—the man who was a minister for over twenty-five years or so. I couldn't hold back the urge to blame my dad for my sisters' homosexuality. I felt it was because of his vulgar acts that were done to my older sister that was the blame for my younger sister's homosexuality. I'm not concluding this as being what I personally believe now; however, learning to feel normal again about everything has been a lifelong experience for me. It feels as if his life and reputation for a very long time had been a black cloud over how I felt about where I come from and who I was. I mean, let's face it: we would all like to have the opportunity of letting someone know how great and important our father is. I suppose the advantage for me was that I was so naive about what he had done. However, not knowing this until adulthood resulted in giving me a false impression of his greatness, allowing me to think and believe in my dad as my idol. It turned out that his deception over me later proved to be healthier for my childhood experience than my sisters.

Later, I sought to understand why the sensuality from men brought uncomfortable feelings in some of my sisters; with my other sisters, it was more of distrust of men and their values and morals. However, as the months and years went by, the reality came to me that my sisters' friendship with their female friends would continue to be permanent for them. At this point, I felt like I was getting more distant from my sisters as time went by. I compared this with having lost something precious or having something taken away and replaced by someone who is now the center of their life. At that time, I must admit that I've never seen them this happy in the past; but back then, I had hoped that it must just be a false sense of happiness that would not last.

As time evolved, I became more of a silent observer of the social lives of my sisters and their friends. I had already said some things about their friends that were out of line, and I had been trying to work on my reputation with them. At that time, I felt a sensation deep down inside that I was a hypocrite because in my heart, I knew that I did not accept my sisters' homosexual life choices. But I pretended to act normal as if nothing was bothering me when I was around them. This is when it became clear to me that my relationship with my sisters was not normal. No one should feel this way around those that are closest to them. Because of this, it came to be a battle for mutual acceptance by both of us. It's a fact that my sisters and I mutually wanted to accept and understand each other's point of view. At that time, I could sense that this process was a dangerous moment in any relationship. Also, I felt as though it could be a time considered as a "point of no return."

I felt that whatever my reaction would be, it would have a lifetime of consequences. What's sad is that most of us don't see that our responses can actually destroy the total relationship. We should consider that what we think and feel about others can change over time. We are constantly changing as people, and our opinions and feelings toward those we are closest to will always be challenged. But our words seem to leave permanent effects—whether it be good words or bad. However, to heal myself I had to understand that it was okay for me to evolve and to have the proper time to adjust from the damage that I've caused similar to this with my one sister.

We must realize that our words and actions can leave permanent damage on others. When someone has caught you in the act of saying or doing something offensive because they are homosexuals, it can be difficult to justify. Also, we don't realize how forgiving yourself can be hard. This becomes necessary because by nature, I think most of us hurt inside when we hurt others. It's just that most don't notice that sometimes the discomfort in our gut and the cloud in our day may come from our missed opportunities to communicate uplifting words, instead of hurting others with our negative statements. I feel that our passion of the moment can deny us the ability to deliver this message to some people when we attempt to express our opinions together with our feelings of pain, anger, and disappointment. From this, we realize that sometimes it's better to say nothing until we make peace with ourselves. If not, our anger usually strikes out at people unintentionally. When this happens, in an effort to justify our actions, some might try to defend themselves, and it can result in our getting caught up in a quicksand situation. The more we struggle to get out, the quicker and deeper we sink.

There were times when I met my sister's friends, and when I did, my curiosity about homosexuals would serve as a temptation for me to ask them multiple questions about their personal lives. I felt as if I needed to study their minds. However, I didn't quite know what I was attempting to find. As time went by, there were things that I would later regret. One of those things, which was later revealed to me, was that one of my sisters felt when we were younger that I was competing with her over some of her girlfriends. I absolutely don't recall this, although I do remember being curious and wondering why they were not attracted to any men. At that time, I did not know that she liked them that way. I thought that my sister's pretty girlfriends were just her regular friends. But it was still uncharted territory for me, and the need that I developed later for me to analyze gay women became a great temptation for my curiosity. I suppose I just wanted to know more about them. Now I must admit that this was the only time that I could truly say that my sisters and I really had something in common. However, her relationship with them was something at that time, which seemed weird to me.

Eventually, I got married. I was one of the first of my siblings to do so. My wife and I quickly began our own family, and years later my two sisters followed and did the same, but the older one married her gay partner that she had known and dated for quite some time. The youngest one married her husband and had kids before later marrying her gay partner. Since then, my sisters have remained "married" to them. At one time, my two gay sisters did not have any relationship or bond with my kids or my siblings' kids and vice versa. So as cousins, they don't really know each other. There's a noticeable difference of how close in touch I am with one sister as compared to the other, although I still love both of them equally.

Nevertheless, I'm not sure what caused my one sister, who is the youngest in our family, to be so different from the other in the way she went about revealing her homosexuality to our family, and her partner was never really formally introduced to me or my family. We've only met her partners a few times—after her first marriage, which was to the father of her kids; and when I met her gay partner, there was a different connection with the way her new spouse and I communicated compared to her husband. Our conversations were noticeably shallow, although I'm not sure what she thought of me, but she seemed as if she definitely wasn't comfortable being around men. I felt guilty of trying to put on my best act when we met. I felt as if I had to analyze my sister and her new spouse every time I was around them. Whenever we met, our conversation was enjoyable. However, it still felt strange to me.

Upon looking back at these encounters, I began to fault myself for the lack of a better relationship with my sisters. It later became clear that most of my other siblings did not have these same issues with homosexuality as I did. I was trying to better understand the differences in my beliefs about homosexuality versus my other siblings, and I was curious to know how they felt. It was kind of different with everyone. As I said earlier, I have one brother who is religiously convicted against homosexuality, while most of my other brothers and sisters' relationship with my two sisters in the beginning began strong but in time became weaker. The reason I think their relationship started out strong was because of everyone's genuine innocent intent in the beginning to have a normal relationship, but over time, the different barriers that divided us were never really dealt with. It must be that everyone seems to just react differently over time.

I believe one of the major problems that we encounter when we are dealing with our anger over someone's life choices normally begin by not knowing how to verbalize our feelings without hurting others. I believe this is more difficult than we think. I also feel this is one of the major problems that plague our relationships today. The fact is that most people are not good at hiding their feelings. Our facial expressions and body language most likely speak for ourselves without any need for words. Most of us lack the ability in being able to conceal the way we feel.

While expressing ourselves, sometimes we become confused in our thoughts and words, which can be influenced by our dislike of someone or something. Take into consideration that it was once socially acceptable to make gay jokes. Now it has become taboo in most of our society today. This is a big leap of progress for those that have been ridiculed most of their lives because of their homosexuality. If we investigate just what motivated this change, one could argue that it is because of this change that we've became compromised in our morals as a society, while others might say that we've become more tolerant, acceptable, and humane. Both sides have compelling arguments, but neither side produces facts that will compel enough to create social harmony in everyone.

Our efforts to help oftentimes hurt others, and as a result, we have less impact in what we seek to accomplish. I think it could be said that we are all seeking to be accepted in one way or another from this world, and when we are not, we all feel that our lives have less meaning. I actually feel that most of us may lack the desire to have compassion for others or to challenge ourselves in this subject. But if others won't be a participant of change, then we must be the leader of this change. Otherwise, we all will continue to be a part of this controversy, whether we like it or not.

As a result of us being for or against homosexuality equality, we will be judged and perhaps ridiculed for what we believe in by others that oppose us. I think that is a common way that most go about in defending their point of view, and it is hurtful and disrespectful to its victims and their freedom of expression. There are things about our belief that are personal to us, and sometimes, I think we expect others to already know and agree with it. We have high expectations of people when we are trying to figure out what they want and who they are. Sometimes we think we know who they are with the little information we know about them, if we know any at all. We have become a society who refuses to take responsibility for being tolerant for people and their beliefs. We feel incomplete if we don't get to remind someone how they should live or what they should believe in.

The reality is that we are vulnerable of false accusations by others, and this creates unnecessary emotional stress for ourselves and others. We all have opinions, and for some people, the pursuit to persuade people to follow their belief is more passionate for some than it is for others. It's been proven that our pursuit to persuade people to accept our beliefs can be nonproductive, especially when we attempt to force-feed our traditions on them. There are some people who feel that if anyone won't change to their way of believing, then there is no other way to relate to them. I believe that our God may have purposely and intentionally designed things in our life this way to deliberately reveal our different reactions, and through this process, it defines how we truly feel in our hearts. Without this opportunity, he would not be able to test our awareness or our imperfections.

Ultimately, I feel that religion played a major part of the blame in most of our family's division over homosexuality, and it still continues today in some ways. It appears that for most, conversations about homosexuality in our families are done more privately. It can be difficult for us to develop that much nerve to be so open with our homosexual dislikes, and perhaps for many of us, it feels more comfortable to talk and express how we really feel when homosexuals are not around. I tried to analyze why I once felt this way. It sort of seemed similar to how others in society acted, I thought. Because of this, I began to feel guilty for what I was doing. The fact was that I really had no words that I could say to my sisters that could adequately express how I felt about them when they were in my presence. However, it seemed that I had no problem when they weren't there. My behavior pattern became disturbing for me, but I felt at that time that it was uncontrollable. What became more disturbing to me was that I could not articulate just how I truly felt in words. If I did attempt to describe how I felt about their homosexuality, I felt a certain doom upon me. *I cannot do this without offending them*, I said to myself. I felt that if I tried to have a normal conversation, doing so would be impossible without me wanting to express what was on my mind about their homosexuality.

Then I realized that maybe I've discovered something. The reasons why most avoid conversations with homosexuals or with others about this topic are fundamentally for the same reasons as I did. I'm not sure if we notice this about ourselves or not. The reality is that most of us will avoid talking about homosexuality, but regardless of this, it can be more revealing how we think and feel by looking at our body language or facial expressions. Sometimes this can be more conspicuous than we imagine. Often, we don't think we can be seen through our smokescreen.

One evening when I was driving my car with my eldest gay sister, she casually asked me how I felt about her homosexuality. This really caught me off guard, but I swiftly bounced back. I used my memories of our childhood as an example of how to express my feelings as I began reflecting on the past and the different experiences then as opposed to the current. Thereafter, being tongue-tied with my first few sentences, I realized that I needed to slow my thought process and try to think more clearly. I began to confirm the difference between my love for her as my sister and my dislike of her being homosexual. I admitted that I had no remedy for this confusion, but I explained that my commitment to continue to love her was a priority to me. After we talked, it seemed to me that she not only understood what I had said but she also supported my thoughts and feelings with compassion. Our relationship as a result began to bloom, and both our families started to become closer because of this. Now my kids and hers know each other, and finally, my immediate family has now successfully developed a relationship with at least one of my sisters and her family.

I began meditating on this and asking myself how much more normal could this be? I finally started to feel differently about my sister's homosexuality. I won't go as far as to say that my religious values still don't tempt me even today to solicit differently. Nevertheless, we must value our relationship so much that we care for it to the point that we are willing to protect it. Of course, that is part of our problem in families and in our society. This act works both ways; I mean that undoubtedly, this seems to be a two-way road. It seems that we categorize the importance of those in the world according to their worthiness to us.

We are critics, whether our views are religious or nonreligious. We stand by what we often say to others, often defending our beliefs with pride instead of compassion. I must admit that when we are trying to express ourselves without hurting others, sometimes we ourselves are harmed in this process. In order for us to expect change, it will take the right desire and passion for those we care for—mixed with the necessary commitment to them—for this to be actually effective. This act of compassion is the foundation that helps relationships to continue to thrive. If we are using ourselves and our faults for our example, then we will realize this to be a more productive way to promote change in others, even if others around us won't change with this process. This can give us more control in how we respond to the most difficult of situations that have become entwined in our lives.

If we understand that forgiveness of others does not mean that we have to surrender our values or morals, but rather that this allows a bridge to exist between us and those that we have chosen to preserve the relationship with, we live another day to work it out. I believe most of us expect change to be immediate, and it could be if we begin with ourselves. I suppose the point I'm attempting to make is that if we dislike anyone because of someone's homosexual lifestyle or if you are a homosexual and dislike those who judge you using most times their religious condemnation. A solution for all of us does indeed exist, and we find that when we are able to forgive those who hurt us, it may not feel as a powerful tool in the beginning. Whether you claim to know God or not, this is a godly act. These things in my opinion define those who are the closest or furthest from a relationship with God. Despite what someone may claim, the results of our actions define who we are. I believe that if we all assess ourselves, this could be used as a better method than judging how others should live. In fact, if we have no expectations of others, then we are not affected by what they do or say.

Also, discovering why we feel this way and finding the correct way to heal without hurting others is the most productive way that yields the most satisfaction. I personally believe that this act and other similar acts would be considered acts of "being normal," and I would argue any aggressive act as being "abnormal," creating abnormal results. In other words, I personally believe that a normal act is based in love, which is of God and multiplies its effects of love. I suppose that becoming "normal" in our lives may require us to embrace the possibility that it will always feel *abnormal.* It will always require us to accept those that we don't like and the many different issues they bring, and eventually, we will realize that possessing great tolerance for others is what defines our morals and uplifts our spirits.

It should be clear by now that there is no satisfaction long-lived in seeing others hurt by what we have said or done. In fact, in most cases, we are disturbed over hurting others, and sometimes we really can't identify what's bothering us. This is when we often seek advice from all sources for help, not really realizing that the answer lies within us through a method of forgiving others. However, there are two parts in this transition.

This is only the beginning of reforming how we personally evolve in our relationship with others. The question may be, how should we as proclaimed believers of God react to the homosexuality of people? My answer again would be to use ourselves as an example. We should always continue examining ourselves constantly for defects instead of being caught in the trap of judging others. Yes, I do consider this a trap because once we start to judge others and their faults as being wrong, it seems to somehow reflect and magnify itself on our lives. We all best serve our interest and the interest in our belief in God, if we magnify those good qualities of others that this by itself will help some to reflect on their bad qualities without our help.

It seems that love is a better motivator for change of others than that of our criticism. Also, it appears that criticism is not the adequate way of dealing with some people that choose to live and act in a way that we feel is wrong. Our motivation could stem from our wanting to be in control over other's lives. I believe that we reach a level of maturity in our quest to "be normal again" when we are no longer seeking others to control but rather seeking personal control over what bothers us as it relates to others that we otherwise would like to control or persuade to change.

I believe that most times, we all instinctively attempt to deal with our adversity in life by using the tools we've learned over time. When we try to create change in others, we overlook to consider ourselves as needing this, not realizing that the missing ingredient to this equation is the necessary changes required within us first. Some may ask, why is this necessary? My answer is based on the fact that we possess the power to inwardly decide good or bad about anyone or anything, and what we say or do will either create positive or stimulate negative results in others whom we seek to change.

It's only logical that we seek to create positive influences as a foundation for our relationships with each other. The method of how we create the change that we expect will only develop from the positive stimulation that we're willing to give. Most times, our negativity or criticism has been proven to persuade its victims to become defensive. Our negative behavior is a threat in nature because it's clear that when we don't accept others, we've caused them to become defensive, and thus, we often miss the opportunity to convince others differently.

In "becoming normal again," it's essential that we must abandon this way of thinking. "Lean not unto your own understanding," says the Word of God. In short, we must learn how to be "normal" while facing abnormal or the-new-normal situations, and while searching to find the tool that will help us all successfully navigate in these uncharted territories of our lives.

4

Who's Judging Whom Now?

In the beginning, the world was already warned. We were all informed about God's directive, which is, "Judge ye not, yet ye be judged." Most of those that have read or heard this scripture most likely never thought of themselves as being the one who is the example of this scripture. Also, some probably felt that their judging of others has its exceptions and is justified somehow from God.

Factually, judging of others has its beginning in heaven. The Bible states that Satan himself is the creator of this, and judgment day was created by God because of Satan's disobedience and the war in heaven that he started. In fact, Satan is considered by God to be the accuser of his brethren, who accused them day and night before God.

Throughout history, mankind's relationship with religion demonstrates a similar pattern as Satan. As a society, we have the tendency to act out judgment as if we are God himself. As individuals, we probably pass judgment on someone on a daily basis, if nothing else but just in our thoughts. In fact, judging is so popular in our society that most everything we do in our culture is established by this method. We've established this learning from our early childhood, starting from when we judge kids' grades to having judges in our sports, and to facing a judge in our courts. Judging of others in our society has become essential. Also, we judge our relationships and even all those whom we love. Most of our marriages and divorces have their beginnings and ends in some sort of judgment of each other.

We actually watch in entertainment as people judge others in some of our popular TV game shows. The point that I'm making should be very clear to you by now: that as a culture, this has become our foundation. We all are guilty of being a habitual judger, for lack of better words. I don't think we as a society have really taken the time to reflect on just how this act is and why it will always be the foundation of our existence. In fact, most worry how they will be judged by others when they die.

I feel that mankind's entire reason for existing on earth is to be judged. If so, the ultimate question then would be, why? Why is judgment so connected with our existence? I feel that everyone being capable to judge each other is one of the key evidences that do prove of an ultimate judgment coming after having lived through so many little judgments by the world. It's sort of like we are being prepared for the ultimate judgment of life that is to come, but the little ones help to prepare us.

When this act of judging was carried out by religious leaders, it has always been considered by most to be accurate about others. Historically, religious condemnation of people was believed by most to be from God when our leaders proclaim it. However, the evolution of religions judging homosexuality in this century has been unlike anything else in our ancient history, partly because of the world media showing the wrongdoings of many religious leaders and followers. Now, religion is at a crossroads with its existence and its power of social influence, partly because of the mistakes from our leaders of the past and present. As a result of this, many have now rebelled in its view of religion.

Those who advocate for homosexuality equality and the pursuit of some to be recognized by the religious community have led and created this movement over time. This has paralyzed the creativity of religious leaders and the ability of followers to effectively represent its traditions and justification for being against homosexual equality. Most religious leaders are often creative in explaining why we need God, but they are not as convincing in their message of why we need to live life the way they believe we should. Religious leaders' most effective tools to justify their beliefs are through the use of Scriptures to judge our actions. Doing this allows the person to come to a conclusion about others using Bible scriptures and other beliefs and deciding what we are violating. This should be easy for most readers to relate to.

As a society and even as followers of our religion, if we would abide by God's law of not judging others, it might lead to us not being judged ourselves. Hopefully from that, we learn that God does a better job at this than the world. In fact, if we're honest with ourselves we would all admit that none of us prefer to be on the other end of this with someone. Once we can recognize that our real power is established in how we accept those that oppose our beliefs, despite feeling that they are not worthy in our view. I believe that this can really be used as a guideline, which will prove to be more productive for us.

I personally believe that God's purpose for mankind possessing this judgment ability was originally intended to be used to self-judge ourselves and not others. As a society, we are misusing this talent that was originally intended to help us keep self-inventory of ourselves. Actually, I really feel this is God's gift to help us abide with Him in spirit. This also gives us the ability to better understand what He expects of us. I believe this is the reason why our Creator has provided us with this built-in judging process that is part of our spiritual makeup, which is also part of how he judges us as well. In other words, God has created all mankind to already know right from wrong. It gives light to the pathway that God has made for us to follow.

Our history demonstrates how religious leaders have used the Bible to judge homosexual behavior in the past using their religious texts to support their claims against it. This sort of religious persecution is similar to those in the Bible of people who were also accused of witchcraft, prostitution, leprosy, adultery, and many other violations of belief supported by Scriptures and religious traditions that some persecutors used. It's proven that our history of religious persecution of others did happen, and it continues until today. However, now we can see more clearly how barbaric things were then. What is horrifying is the thought that those who carried out such acts with many people did so with what it seemed was no compassion for others or for life.

Our religious traditions and beliefs have always played the dominant role in mankind's justification for its judging and persecution of others. It seems that our beliefs have not fundamentally changed but have evolved by splintering off into many different denominations centered around the same belief that God is our Creator and the Creator of the world. Our different religious traditions today have had their origins well before anyone alive today was conceived. In fact, we are all followers of ancient traditions established before our great-grandparents' parents. Our ideas are not original or authentic; rather, they are ongoing traditions and beliefs discovered and practiced by many others who lived thousands of years before us. Basically, we judge others today based upon opinions, traditions, and belief of others before us. Although history has proven that there have always been unnecessary death and destruction caused by our traditions and beliefs, we continue to consider these facts as being irrelevant in our attempt to serve mankind.

Homosexuals and their claims that our religious leaders and followers are wrong for their condemnation of their life choices are not unique in our history, contrary to what some may think. The Bible was not written recently just to interfere with our life choices, but it has always been the authority for our social and moral order. Our religious leaders and followers of today are being blamed by those who oppose our religious ideology, knowing that they did not create it. Actually, religious believers are only teaching what they have learned, which is something that was established before any of us were thought of. Although it has been proven by history that religious persecution has a dark and bloody past and that everything done by our leaders was not always what God may have wanted, but because of our history, it has indeed been proven that as a society, we are similar to those from the past. From this, we realize that we have all prejudged or condemned others. Furthermore, I think we can relate to this because in some way, we are all guilty ourselves sometimes of the same offenses.

As our society has changed from one generation to the next, it seems to be more common that the newer generation wants to do things differently than before, and each generation seems to feel the desire of renovating our old traditions. Our religious traditions are one of the last foundations that represent our belief in religion, and now it faces judgment of its own. It seems that the very foundation that has established our morals and belief is now losing its ability to influence. By this, a question could be asked by some: why is this? In answering, I'm sure we would have many different opinions. The fact is that we somehow did evolve from what we were to who we are now, and our religion has always been used as a guideline for our social and moral order.

The fact that this newer generation of our society views religious traditions much differently than the generations of times past and that our religious leaders have not been able to reshape their message have caused this effect to intensify. The birth of alternative religions has been proven to be competitive to our old beliefs. There are new religious views that are more accepting of homosexuals but that represent God in ways much different than that which traditional religion teaches. Their religious belief is more tolerant of others than what is ordinarily taught, and their message is rising in popularity with those who attend. It seems that today our religious leaders have either backed away entirely from the subject of how God declares homosexuality to be wrong, or they go to the extreme in their message of God condemning homosexuals to hell.

Also, it appears as if there is not much compassion from anyone when we don't agree on this subject. With most people, it's either we agree with each other or we put up our walls of defense and declare war. It seems that we could have compassion for others, and we all should recognize that we are not the person that created these traditions that oppose people's views. But with the right compassion and concern, we can be the generation that can create harmony, as we are dealing with this subject to create greater tolerance in our religion and in our society.

Sometimes, in our efforts to defend what we believe, we often try with great effort to make our point clear to others regarding how we feel and think. We are quick to judge their beliefs or traditions. Our opposition that we take on with some people over their opposing opinions and beliefs has often caused us to ignore vital views that others may have, when they are opposing our beliefs. We sometimes defend what we believe, as if we never can be wrong or as if it is always the other person that is not correct. In fact, when most leaders of "homosexual equal rights groups" and "religious authority" are both debating issues, most do so in a war-like atmosphere. Over time, both have proven to be unproductive in creating any major change in our society that will bring together our relationships and differences regarding religion and homosexuality.

It seems that both sides of this debate and their foundations for their belief are supported by the way each side interprets the Scriptures. Both have used biblical scriptures that they claim support their views and establish proof that the other is wrong. From this fact, we can determine that one of these opposing opinions cannot be correct. It's also clear that the Scriptures have been misunderstood before, and this serves as further proof that it can be done again. However, someone's interpretation of the Scriptures may not always be factual. Sometimes, opinions of Scriptures can differ from those of the same belief. I suppose trying to change the scriptural interpretation of God's Word in a way that is fair to all our views might seem impossible, but this does demonstrate why it is necessary now for our religious leaders and followers to adapt and lead more boldly, to lead with new methods while teaching others about the traditional messages.

There is an obvious disconnect in our message of God's love and tolerance for others and of who is considered by Him to be worthy or not of his eternal life. The problem our religious leaders face today is proving to nonbelievers that God, who loves all, is also capable of such compassion for all. Somehow, some that oppose religion and its followers created the thought that those living today actually unfairly came up with this idea against the world, using the Bible to condemn the life choices of everyone. Others may believe that most of our religious leaders will only focus on the part of God's law that speaks of judgment for the sins of others, instead of the part that promises us of His love, salvation, patience, and long-suffering as being important. Also, it's not taught that homosexuals are able to equally acquire His grace as others do. Most importantly, what is not spoken about often enough is that we don't patiently wait for others to develop, as they are still learning about God.

We must consider that if we are actually seeking to stop anyone from living the way they wish to live, that is not what God intended for us to do. God made all of us with the freedom of choice. The Bible gives clarity to the fact that God did not restrict mankind's choice of the way we choose to live our lives, even our choice of self-destruction. I feel that as a society, no one has the permission or authority *but* God, and if He designed mankind without restrictions to make his or her own life choices, good or bad, then I would question why anyone else should be able to make that type of decision for others. It seems that we act out of our good intentions when we try to stop someone's freedom of choice, but the idea that we consider ourselves doing the work of the Almighty should be questionable when He himself has never put such restrictions on man's ability to make such choices.

I believe that our life choices that we choose to live actually helps God with His decision-making for the day of judgment when the Lord essentially makes his ultimate choices about mankind himself at that time. The less freedom that mankind has to make choices in their life, the more it limits God's ability to know the results of who we really are. We should not restrict anyone from their choice, especially if it does not hurt or endanger anyone. If our Creator does not require that of mankind, then why should we require it of others? There was a reason why the Almighty purposely allowed His creation *the freedom of choice*, and He demonstrates in Scripture why we do not have the authority to require anything different of others. We are only required to teach others the message from Scriptures and not enforce it.

Maybe our good intentions to help and our frustration that we feel when others ignore what seems perfectly clear to us helps enforce our radical opinions about the way someone lives their life. We must consider that if we are trying to live as an example of how others should live, then we must realize how humble Jesus Christ's approach always was to those whose life choices were controversial. In fact, Jesus defended a prostitute from being stoned to death while declaring to those who were about to stone her, "To whom that is without sin, let them cast the first stone." Our Lord's ability to show love for unpopular people of society allowed for others to transform their opinion about Jesus and His teachings because of how His approach had such intensive compassion, as it applies to the life choices of people that contradict our traditions. Jesus Christ's attitude was more appealing to others than the religious leaders of that time, who were quicker to condemn others in God's name. Most of them felt as if they had a greater right to judge others, more so than Jesus Christ did. Ironically, it seems that history does continue to repeat itself, and the judging of men in God's name continues to exist with us today.

This history should help us to remember that ultimately, Jesus himself was judged by the religious leaders of His day, who claimed that what He said was blasphemy when He declared Himself as the son of God. This offense is one of the claims that led Him to the cross. We must remember that the elite religious leaders of that time are responsible for their wrong accusations of Jesus Christ. They in fact probably thought that they had good intentions in their thinking, that persecuting Jesus was defending God himself. This should serve as a perfect example, and it demonstrates the way mankind continues to misinterpret the Scriptures. The problem could be solved very easily if we all clearly understood that we are wrong when we act out our religious condemnation on others. Of course, that would be simple for us if it could be done, but the fact is that we don't have that luxury as an option. Therefore, this requires us to analyze everything carefully before we come to a final judgment of others. We should use how Christ was judged as our example of how leaders were incorrect at the time in their persecution of Him. When using this as an example, it should give us more of a reason to always question ourselves and our reasons for the opinions that we have of others.

The question for some in our society should be: Why do we view our religion and our God as being outdated and obsolete, or why we do not desire to follow God's Word? We are the generation that has evolved for over thousands of years since Jesus Christ's death, and we see things differently now than those before us. The big question is why. Why now are we going against the Bible and religion because it judges us? It has always judged generations before us. When we blame our religious leaders and followers today of their religious judgments and their hypercritical persecution of others, we are making them responsible for something much bigger than they are.

If we were better able to understand more about how we judge others and how religion judges homosexuality, then we will begin to learn that this is indeed part of mankind's nature. We all try to use our best facts to defend this point, even though history has proven this act to be unproductive, particularly when trying to solicit religion to someone. This tactic is used sometimes when we are finding the faults of others in the world; it seems to justify what we do. Maybe it is used by us to cover what we do not wish to see in ourselves. When we judge others, it's a hurtful thing to our victims. But if we use this for ourselves, it will be the tool that will bring us closer to a clearer understanding of who we are.

It's not unusual in today's world to witness people who use the Bible as a justification to judge other's lifestyles. Most that do are likely to eventually encounter a rebellious conflict. There are many today that won't tolerate religious judgment of their lives, and because of this, I personally think that those that feel this way could have been tolerating the judgment of others for many years of someone or something that has tried to define them against their will. I think that this does not necessarily mean it has to be religious judgment that's responsible by itself, but economic and social conditions tend to be a factor for us. In fact, it appears that religion has been influenced by its fallen leaders that cross over to just about every segment of our society. If this could be used as our example, we would see that the fallen leaders in our society are further proof of how no one is above religious condemnation of this world. It also should serve as additional evidence of how we should not rely on others as examples for how we should live when we do this. We begin to realize how we have been allowing ourselves to be led by other men and women that are vulnerable to mistakes, just as we have been.

Most people that oppose religion and its followers don't actually realize that the religion these fallen leaders represent existed before the leaders began and will continue to exist when they're gone. The question is: should we blame the leaders of religion for not doing as their belief or tradition says, or should our blame be on God who is the author of the religion, or both?

I suppose I'm suggesting that if we are upset at religious leaders for what they believe and teach, then that would be where the term "Don't shoot the messenger" would apply; the messenger himself is just delivering the message. If we're not mad at God, then it seems as if our anger is on those that believe in him. I feel it's helpful to better understand if we are mad at religious leaders, religion, or God. It's good to know what's really bothering us.

After having witnessed many fallen leaders go through their downfall, I began to understand some things about religion more clearly. One of those things was how no one is above others or no one is perfect but God. Also, the deception to do wrong exists with our leaders and in high places of society as well. Understanding this allowed me to use this information as an example of why looking upon others for our religious guidance can be misleading for everyone involved. When religious leaders do wrong, it seems that others lose faith in God. It's almost as if God takes the blame for things for what others that represent Him do, while really He has done nothing at all. It also appears as if some of us expect more of our Creator than He will give. In taking all this into consideration, it is as if we are judging God ourselves when we do this. Our anger may exist with Him more so than man, who only attempts to follow. Fundamentally, it seems that we have the ability to overpower man when we oppose earthly things, but how anyone can overpower God and dispute his Word after our death has proven to be more elusive.

If it's the truth that we seek, I'm puzzled as to why there are efforts by some to alter or misinterpret the true meaning of the Scriptures. I'm sure all is not done so purposely by others, but more so out of their good intentions that end up being reckless. However, sometimes our opposing views of others can turn reckless when we attempt to alter the facts of other people's views that we disagree with. We actually end up being counterproductive in our pursuit to influence anyone, especially if we're expecting to persuade people by our example. When religious leaders are condemning anyone using the Scriptures, they usually all have different views of the very same Scriptures. Part of our flaws in our traditions is that some of these beliefs are made up by man and are imperfect. Many of these traditions were established as a result of mankind's interpretation of the Bible, whether it was what God actually intended or not.

When we attempt to eradicate something, you usually start from its source. Leaders and believers of religion, who judge others for their homosexuality, receive their source of information from the Scriptures of their Bibles. Therefore, we must know if we seek to stop the religious leader; we must first stop the Bible from being believable. Actually, what we really are asking for is everyone not to have an opinion about their religion or forcing our religious leaders to actually be untruthful about facts of the Bible when they teach about their belief. Our actions say that we don't want anyone to teach the truth as they see it. Actually, we are avoiding certain realities that we disagree with and are seeking to destroy the foundation in which it stands because of our disagreement. The truth is that religion and its roots date back thousands of years before any of us, and it doesn't seem logical to me that anyone has the superior knowledge to claim that we are wiser than those before us or that we have the right to change anything. I feel that we should always seek to maintain and value all of our ancient history and this is demonstrated with our many artifacts from the past that have been preserved in museums. It shows that as a society, we understand the importance of preserving our past traditions and beliefs for future generations to learn from.

If we change, it does not always mean that everything else always has to change to accommodate us. If we expect others to respect our decision to live how we want, then the question becomes: How can we expect to limit others of their freedom of what to believe or not as well? It's just logical thinking that sounds fair if you're equally dividing something up.

There are those in positions of religious authority who have been responsible in the false condemnation of others, even until recent history. It was unthinkable in most cases to accuse them of something wrong. Of course, we know today that this type of thinking in the past is what allowed for those individuals to go unnoticed. However, what I could never understand is how most of these individuals appeared to be so intelligent and yet were so naive about who God is, or at least understanding of what morals were. It seems that most of them even forgot that they are the example for others and should live the way that they teach.

In our society, we've had fallen teachers, preachers, politicians, and public servants of every kind—all of who have failed society, their family, God, and themselves. What I wonder is how does one who judge others do so while being aware of their own personal demons. How can their feeling of superiority over others exist in them, especially if they are aware that it's all just a show for the world to see? I often wonder how could there be some that say they know God, when they know deep down inside that they're guilty themselves of things? It's amazing to wonder if they feel anything, and how do they justify it? I also believe that most people today are beginning to see things happen this way so often, that at times, they may think that this is normal.

It's a fact that the world has always judged others throughout our history, and this is not unique in our evolution. However, even in an advanced society such as ours, this ancient act still exists, despite all it's done for man throughout history which only has cause wars, death and conflict. I believe that this is an underrated act that until now hasn't been on anyone's radar. It's an intangible act that has tangible results. This act of judging was used as an instrument needed by establishments with the purpose of maintaining social or religious order, but it quickly became contagious. Over the years, it has evolved into our society as being needed in almost everything we do. If we dare to examine the act of judging, we will find some fundamental facts that might not have been considered before, until now.

In order for someone to condemn another about their life choices or things they have done, it requires for the person doing this to be totally acting as if they are a god when doing so. We act like we own this power to have our opinions of others, and by doing this, we eventually begin to have pride in ourselves. We cannot escape this power. It almost comes as a package deal: power equals pride. The problem then becomes: how does one identify when pride has compromised their thinking and ability to come to conclusions fairly of what we believe of others? In fact, I don't believe that most of us would actually take inventory of ourselves to guard against our being compromised by pride. Nevertheless, it probably happens less than we would imagine.

The act of pride is an underrated enemy against our being able to have social justice for all. There is no system that is designed that can detect when others act unfairly out of their self-righteousness. It can even fool us into believing that we are not that way ourselves, even when we clearly are. Of course, the pride of Satan in heaven is where this originated, and it was used by Satan as he magnified himself against God and all the others that existed in heaven. Satan is the one who created pride and is the owner of this act that was created in heaven. When we are acting out this way, we are actually recreating this act (that originally began with Satan). We are sucked in by its power. It always has been seductive to mankind. Those that are in high positions of authority cannot escape its power, and even those in low positions benefit from its power to seduce us.

The original intent for our having the ability to be proud was to be used as a feeling that we have for others, not ourselves. This gift was given to us by God to help others. Having pride in others serves to benefit this world more than it does when we use it for self-pride. It then makes sense of the real intent designed by God for the use of it when we use pride to uplift others with our praise. It becomes an extension of love to others and gives more reason for life for the recipient of it, and when pride is used to reflect ourselves as being better—it represents a selfish and self-centered way to become. The fact that most people who operate under so much of it and are not aware of it, demonstrates further how most have become so intoxicated by their self-pride that it's impossible for them to see the greatness of anyone else. In fact, those individuals sometimes become so unaware of their circumstance that despite what they do, it really becomes a sad story once we learn more about how lonely most become as they have excluded or destroyed most relationships of those that did care for them at one time.

Understanding that our leaders are human and that they will make mistakes themselves should give further reasons why we all should be led by our own research of information and not by anyone else. Although there is value in our leaders and the many different things that are useful for us that they teach, knowing what to learn from our leaders of what is useful information or not can be elusive. Our common sense should help us when we are faced with these kinds of decisions. Sometimes we are so impressed with others that we fail to understand that they indeed have flaws as we do. The point I'm attempting to make is that there will always be preachers and teachers that we are impressed with, but we must always consider that they have issues about them that are not obvious yet. At first it can be hard for us to imagine someone that we're so influenced by who is not perfect.

It is important to understand the self-centered condition that people operate with while under the influence of their self-pride. They are not reflecting on anyone else, only their world and what is important in that circle of theirs. Their leadership of others can be compromised if discretion in their decision-making is not used properly. In other words, because of being self-righteous, they don't see clearly.

Our condemnation of people takes place in ordinary life with those we encounter every day. We are constantly making judgment of others and of the situations that we face. This may be the reason for the phrase "judge of good character," which comes from when we meet someone for the first time. As I've said in the beginning of this chapter, God did warn man not to judge. He mandated this rule for a reason, and I believe that today's society is a reflection of what God was trying to prevent.

Again, this skill of judging if used for ourselves would be most effective for us as it relates to knowing when to have caution in our judgment before being critical of others. Being able to control our God-given talent of judging, whether it's of others or of ourselves, can be a sign of our maturity. It reveals to God and to others who we truly are. I guess the line we cross is when we begin to feel as if we are more entitled than others, and they are less deserving to whatever it may be. For anyone to come to a self-indulged conclusion that others are not as deserving might be experiencing an attack on their common sense. Even if we claim that our lives are more significant than God's creation of animals or birds, the question then becomes, whose opinion are we using to form that conclusion, and does our creator share this opinion? I mean, "God's eyes are on the sparrow" as well, as the Bible states. His creation of other life is precious, just as mankind's, isn't it? This pattern of thinking is another example of how we judge everything of this world. We categorize things by the priority of its usefulness or worthiness as we perceive it to be, but does God view his creation the same way as mankind does?

If we were to consider our existence in life as limited with time and everything on earth as being temporary, then all things that exist are merely coming to earth and then leaving with short life spans; even we ourselves are just here temporarily. From this, we would better understand that this evolving door of life has its cycle that continues over and over, and it has continued for thousands of years from the time of the ancient civilizations until the present day. It's been proven that no one person or civilization will indefinitely control what others will do in future generations. Although we do evolve from past traditions, mankind has uniquely changed in ideas and values throughout each generation. In fact, the more I begin to absorb the fact of how insignificant we are when we consider the thousands of years of civilizations that have come and gone before us, the more I question how any of us can expect to feel that we are somehow more precious or special than the others who have lived before us or those that are yet to come.

I believe that our act of judging others might change when we understand life from this point of view. The perspective of "who are we to judge anyway?" seems so foolish after witnessing people who judge others while later being found unworthy to lead by example themselves. There are also those that can see everyone's faults but their own, although these are more obvious and extreme examples. It does, however, highlight the point I'm trying to make, and that is: our opinion and our lives may be important to us, but it is really insignificant when we consider and compare them to others before us. Even the civilizations thousands of years before us whose influences strongly shaped the world have come and gone. Nothing is permanent in terms of man's control over others, and man's unfair judgment of others will always coexist with us. This should give some clarity to my point, which is: our society will always continue to redefine itself throughout each generation.

Most may not think that the hurt and pains they have caused in other people's lives have consequences. It's more common for us to tell others what we feel is wrong with them or offer our advice on what they should do. We never consider what pain and stress we have inflicted on them. In fact, some delight in any process to hurt people and do so with intent, neglect, and lack of conscience. When we no longer allow others and how they live their lives affect us, it would be a big beginning for us. The fact that we are still able to find a way to show compassion for others even if we don't agree with them is one method of how we might find the remedy for what bothers us most. I mean, think this through: if we actually dealt those we hate with love, it would not only redefine who we are but it could also work as a method in finding joy while successfully associating with those that we would not otherwise.

I believe this is one of the ways in which we all can begin the process to stop ourselves from condemning people. It usually begins with knowing why we become negative about our victims without a fair analysis of facts. We will justify our actions pretty well. We can fool ourselves better than we do anyone else when we do this, and our negative opinions of others always have the opposite effect of what we intended. Most don't realize how it does not motivate others to change, as we may assume. In fact, most of the time, it brings about the opposite effect of what was intended by us.

If we evaluate ourselves, we might find that most of us have never considered that condemning others for how they live could actually affect us personally or that it is capable of slowly stealing our joy away. In fact, most of us might consider it a duty to judge others daily. It's probably not a popular idea that we can find joy from overlooking the things that others do that we consider to be wrong. Most of us will not miss the opportunity to give someone advice when their lives have become unmanageable or to act like God by judging how others should live. It seems that we always are comparing ourselves as being much better than others by virtue of our morals and values or material gains, usually possessing a feeling that we have authority over others because of our certain beliefs. We have never stopped to consider how doing this does in fact affect our happiness and our ability to have compassion for everyone. We can only experience this peace when we have concern for others before considering ourselves. If we do this, it will hurt us when we hurt others. If we cannot feel any emotions when we hurt others, then it is a sign of our inability or weakness to love. This awful feeling that we get when we are hurting others was meant for all of humanity to be guided by.

In fact, it is my belief that when we reserve our judgment of others, not only do we receive more inner peace but we also preserve the power of influence that we have with them. It can inspire some to self-analyze themselves as a direct result with our doing this. So what I'm trying to say is that reserving our judgment of others and replacing it with thoughts of love and compassion is actual therapy from us. I mean, we could absorb this energy easier than having bad feelings because of people we are trying to correct. Most don't realize the values and benefits that come to us from treating others with dignity. We actually think there is value in correcting people or being an authority for how the world should live. The point is that having this type of thinking comes with a feeling of frustration that is guided by disappointment because we feel the need to see others differently.

I think our challenge will be finding how we turn off this kind of desire to expect others to be what we think they should be, and learning how we can influence others to change—without creating frustration for ourselves and for them. I believe that the solution will come from the patience and compassion that we are all capable of showing to others. The thought that this could actually be therapeutic to us is what should get everyone's attention. Sometimes the most unlikely thing that can solve our problem is what ends up being the thing that actually helps us.

Our success is determined by the end results of everything we do and how we dealt with it. Everyday life presents itself again with new challenges. We reshape our future by our daily decisions. Those who oppose us will always exist as well as those we oppose, whether it's only over tedious matters or other matters of greater importance. The fact of how we make it through this process is what will ultimately define who we are and the direction of our future. The road that is best for us is usually the one that seems to be at first the most difficult to travel or something impossible for us to do. In fact, if we need help in making a decision about what we do with others that do wrong to us, we should pick the challenge that does require more of us. We should automatically know that to stand for good, our experience will be similar to Jesus Christ and his judgment that He experienced from the world.

5

Learning How to Love Religious People

It has been said before that religious people can be the most difficult ones to love, and it's okay to feel this way. I probably would be the first to admit as a religious believer that there are some that claim religion while most others can see that they are still struggling in trying to live out their religious beliefs. In fact, most can be very different and complex because of what is believed in their religion. Oftentimes, one's religion is the only example of how they should live. I believe we're driven by the need to share with others things that are new and exciting about our life. It's sort of the same thing with our religious belief. In explaining our belief to others, we feel we have something to offer of importance. Also, we are driven by our excitement to share our new discovery with those that we meet. However, this is when the beginning of most of our problems occurs: by just attempting to share our religious beliefs or personal views with others. This is when most will try to influence others of the way they should live when they do this. Most never reflect on how they might appear to their recipient when they're promoting their religion, or why their attempt to reenact what ultimately persuaded their belief; it often ends in failure when trying to influence this to others.

Most that try to influence people about their religious belief have never seriously considered themselves as the one who is an example of what they confess to those that they solicit their message to. Most religious people are committed in what they believe, but they are not totally educated in everything about their belief. I have found that most religious people base their belief on a few fundamental issues about the religion that persuaded their personal belief. However, I think that if everyone were quizzed on it, most would fail in understanding the basic facts of their religion. That is proof of how believers have been led into a belief without considering all details about it. I am not saying that religious believers in general are unknowledgeable about their religion, but that many are convinced about a concept of something that they are not able to explain as convincingly as they believe.

I think the puzzle-like effect of trying to learn everything about religion is strategically designed by God to be conspicuous from us, and it can only be understood better as someone's relationship matures with Him. The majority of religious believers are unaware that on a day-to-day basis, there are always new things to learn. Most feel that they have already maximized what can be learned about their religion, not realizing how much more knowledge there still remains to be learned. Often, this is more apparent when we fail in trying to be the example for what we confess to believe. It's essential that we understand that whatever we do or don't do will remain controversial to some and will lead to criticism by others that don't agree. Nevertheless, an essential part of appreciating someone's traditions and beliefs is when we realize that we have things in common with them despite our differences.

It's a fact that belonging to a particular religion might create controversy within our very own religious community or our families. This is because some have different interpretation of the Scriptures and other beliefs, and as a result, many differ in opinions. Therefore, some people feel that their doctrine is superior or more authentic. However, having these different beliefs is not unique. The interpretation of doctrine has always caused great religious division, resulting in the creation of different denominations of believers. However, common sense should lead us into believing that not all these traditions and beliefs are authentic.

It's likely that the world will never fully understand the different religions and what they represent or realize that this is what helps to maintain our religious divide. In fact, attempting to learn the entire world's different concepts of who God is might cause the brain to go in information overload. This gives better clarity to me of how mankind must be careful with its choice in religion and also in those that lead. It's clear that the world is not united in their belief of God and the traditions that are intended for us. There are many beliefs that must be fundamentally incorrect, but the big religious debate becomes, which ones are? This is often when we all began to criticize each other for our different religious beliefs.

So whether mankind chooses any religion or not, doing so will still leave us open to criticism by someone regarding what we believe. The point that I'm hoping to establish is that whether mankind is religious in belief or not, we all tend to criticize or condemn people that we don't agree with. In fact, we as a society are so self-centered in our thinking that we don't allow others to be different from us on almost anything that conflicts with our beliefs and traditions. We are disorganized with our thinking when it requires for us to change anything about ourselves or our values, especially family traditions that are handed down from generations before us. Most religious believers are usually led to their beliefs by the influence of someone else. We form our opinion with great trust and belief, absent of facts which cannot be accurately verified by us in most cases, because whatever we choose to believe originated thousands of years before any of us were ever born.

If we are honest with ourselves, we would have to admit that our religious beliefs come with limited knowledge of whom God is and how the creation of man and Earth began with God, but it certainly does not provide proof of how our spirit within us came to be created by God as well. We all have our different opinions about the creation of earth and mankind, whether we share the same religion or not. No one has a factual explanation that everyone has been mutually able to clearly agree with. Our belief is limited with how religion actually started and who started it. There are so many versions of whom and what God is that understanding all of it becomes elusive. Most religious believers' level of education in religion is limited. We rely on others to explain thoroughly what the important parts of the Bible and other religious texts really mean and without a pastor or leader, most believers of religion would be in a state of confusion. This serves as proof of why we rely on some of our leaders for guidance.

When we follow certain religious beliefs and after learning about a specific concept of what religion and God is, it seems that we attach ourselves to that belief and solicit others using the same methods of how we learned. Most religions that are converting others to their beliefs do so with the philosophy that "once we believe, it's our duty to teach it to others." Educating people in this way of believing is always done so with the awareness that it is something that has been passed down from thousands of years of traditions of others before us, and what we learn can be as different as the many beliefs that exist for us to learn.

However, it would revolutionize the world if an entire library of information on different religions could be learned without having to educate ourselves about these religions. If it were possible to do this, most of us would not have accomplished learning this amount of education in our lifetime. To realize that in reality we actually rely on very limited facts for us to form our opinions on such a gigantic topic as religion should actually be a sobering thought for us. I'm certain most people think that their preference of religion was because of a choice they made after having understood all other concepts of religion. When in fact, our knowledge about religion is limited and usually influenced out of what we learned when we were young or from those that are close to us who introduced us to their religion. The purpose of explaining this is to expose how most of us aren't fully educated about what we believe. Despite this, some are willing to defend their point with others, even if it guaranteed their death. When we defend our beliefs and traditions, it's often done with a lack of concern about the details of the beliefs of others.

This is when it gets confusing because it's a God that we all worship who has already given the world its directive, which is "to love others as we love ourselves." It is a priority commandment for us. Yet it seems as if we do the opposite, especially with those who do not agree with our traditions or beliefs. It's obvious that most don't consider that when they do this, we are a living example of what we believe. There are some who actually think that they know who God wants to punish and feel that they have the right to act for Him. But God teaches us to "love one another" as being one of our Creator's greatest commandments, just under the commandment of loving Him first. Despite this, we seek for ways to overlook the most important expectations of His written Word, and we continue to condemn others.

What we don't consider is the fact that the religious values we do believe when we did learn about it, more than likely was not a thought out process that lead us into becoming part of that religion. In fact, there were other convincing elements about that religion that convinced us to believe. When most of us discover a religion, our choices are sometimes made suddenly and done with a sense of excitement. We embrace new things about the religion that we believe were amazing and overlook necessary research that might otherwise have changed our opinions had we known differently. Once we've made a decision about a religion, it is usually because of how comfortable we feel or that we sense a certain connection. Sometimes it can be because of how we were welcomed, or maybe because of how our loved ones have been changed by this experience. There can be many reasons that serve as a bridge for us to pass over the vital facts that would otherwise influence our decision. The fact is that we're faced with trying to understand thousands of years of different beliefs in a short time. It is an important example of how our religion has always been decided this way, and understanding this does begin to make better sense when we are examining where we are today in our religious society.

Most religions are more effective in teaching their message of our need to love others, but they fail to be clear on exactly how to do this or the effective way to be tolerant of those opposing our views. The point I'm attempting to make is that most religions and their traditions build their foundations on love, tolerance, and forgiveness. Also, in this teaching, we have no biblical justification for enforcing our condemnation on others. In biblical times, Jesus had defended a prostitute from being stoned to death by a mob of people and is quoted as saying, "Those without any sin, may they cast the first stone," when He was defending the woman against the mob. The fact that they stopped in their attempt to stone her was only the result of Jesus challenging those to judge themselves the same as they are judging her. The mob I'm sure did not stop stoning her in fear of Jesus or what He would do, but rather because of a result of their personal inventory that they conducted as Jesus suggested.

If we really believe that our intentions to follow our religion are genuine, then we should live life as that example. We would have to agree that Jesus Christ's way of not judging others is consistent with that example of how we should live and treat people. Most might consider it to be that individual's personal penalty that they deserve while seeing someone being stoned by a mob. Many of us would not intervene in fear of what the mob might do to us. In fact, some of us might throw a few stones ourselves if we had the chance. This should serve as our example that our purpose is better served by being like Jesus in the way that He would protect and care for others that differ from His beliefs. In fact, He directly challenges this mob to take inventory of themselves and their motives as an example, and it actually was Jesus Christ's point to this mob, and it is meant to be the priority for our lives as well. Although all the laws of God are not as clear as the Ten Commandments are, God still leaves plenty of clues in what may be considered as insignificant stories of the Bible that we overlook and fail to take clues from.

This story demonstrates why we should analyze and use ourselves as an example before judging others. I think God made it clear of his dissatisfaction in our religious persecution of others. This example of Jesus Christ and of the mob that attempted to stone this lady was purposely written for us today, not just to hear of this great story but also to purposely serve as an example to mankind of how to live and how to treat others that live outside the tradition of our religious beliefs. When we consider that this mob did not throw a single stone after analyzing their past, this is proof that the mob realized that they were wrong for attempting to kill her. Jesus made a strong point to the mob of how to judge themselves first before stoning this lady. This really depicts how God wants us to think. The point God clearly was trying to make to us is how important it is to judge ourselves instead of others. It further illustrates what our priorities should be when it comes to how we think about others.

Although, Jesus Christ doesn't elaborate much on why He has compassion for those that don't follow Him or those that live the opposite of what He teaches, our Lord still extends His forgiveness for them and His grace, further demonstrating how He is despite our differences. When Jesus Christ does this, it's clear that He was not angry at this lady for the way that she has not listened and followed the religious laws, and He is not offended because she is not a follower of His belief. The majority of our religious believers would not have done the same as Jesus did. Most of us would have concluded that she was not a follower of our tradition and would also support the thought that she must deserve to be stoned. Before Jesus defended her, it was clear how angry this mob's mentality of thinking was, and it highlights their deep desire to kill her. It also further illustrates how, even today, we are quick to judge and persecute others.

I believe in this story, Jesus is able to convince others to use themselves as the example to motivate better choices. It also demonstrates how we have not allowed these facts to become a common-sense concept for us today, although we may or may not understand exactly what the mob's thoughts was. What we can confirm is that when we are letting others live with our forgiveness, we are able to expect forgiveness from God as well. If we have a heart of compassion than this will serve as a method to tighten our relationship with God, and as a way to obtain a peaceful relationship with others that we otherwise would not. What is worth noting is that in this story it appears that the mob is not trying to stone her because she had done anything to them personally, but rather because what she was doing was a violation of their belief. It also shows how we can be led to anger and so quickly influenced by our moral values. Sometimes we feed off other people's suspicions and fears. I'm sure the mob started with just a few that were angry and who solicited others in joining in their campaign. This is proof of how we can be led to condemning people without fully knowing the facts. We sometimes put our trust in what others' points of views are, without first investigating the facts for ourselves. This crowd actually had no fear of being part of a murder of someone, and as a mob, they felt more justified.

Although getting someone today to participate in the killing of others might be somewhat different compared to the laws back then and also compared to those times of Jesus Christ, the fact remains that we all instinctively carry this same personality trait. Maybe our intentions are not to necessarily kill those that are different from us, but we certainly need to examine ourselves just as Jesus asked those that were about to stone her to do. It appears that maybe this is a point or process that has been overlooked by most of us today—that is, realizing that God has already given us this example as our guide. I believe that following this belief reveals our true nature of who we are. It's easier for us to see what we don't like in others, but we're not usually so successful in being capable of seeing the same things in ourselves. I believe that we all begin with our innocent intentions when attempting to do what we feel God would want us to do when we act out our condemnation on others for their lifestyles. Our problem is in not believing that we are in need of the same considerations that we impose on others and not realizing that unless we actually start analyzing ourselves, our understanding will be limited.

I believe that most of us that attend religious services have experienced how some of its members can be disrespectful and sometimes hateful that it can make anyone wonder, "Why do they come to church at all?" In fact, if we go often enough and long enough, we will have the opportunity to witness other things about some church members that should make you question other people's intentions regarding religion. I honestly believe that as religious followers, we can be the hardest to love at times. Also I feel that we are conditioned to be against what is *not* of God, as some might say. Everything we do, we attempt to claim whether it is *of* His will or not. Although we may not use these same requirements for the way we guide our lives, we often think others should believe what we value to be from God himself. We begin to feel that we are entitled to condemn, and it's as if we start living our life and using ourselves as an example for others to live.

In the church that I attend, there is a member who always greets me with an insult every time I see her in church. She has done this to me and most of my family members throughout the years. It almost seems that her insults are done inconspicuously. When she insults you, she will do it with such an innocent smile that sometimes I'm confused as to whether she intended it to be an insult or not. Personally, I feel she is the perfect example of how I learned to care for the toughest that there is who claims to be a religious person. Trying to understand her motivation for being this way at first seemed to be what was important to me, but over the years I just acted as if I ignored her derogatory comments. Although she was successful in getting some of my relatives to stop coming to this church because of her offensive comments to them; despite this, my wife and I today continue to attend. It's not as if we ignore *her* but rather her comments. I don't know if she has a problem or if that's how she is naturally; but nevertheless, she is an example of the many personalities of religious believers that we will encounter. In the beginning, it felt as if maybe God was testing my ability to be patient. It made no sense that I should have to deal with people like this in my own church, but I had to realize that even going to church does not exclude us from experiencing what everyday people do, and it does not shield us from the things they do.

I used this example with the intent to illustrate how trying to love religious people is no different than trying to love those that are not and how understanding both is complex. One of the things that divide us are our different beliefs and traditions as well as our experiences of life. In our evolution of religion before the death of Jesus and until modern times, our leaders and followers of religion have disagreed with one another on our religious beliefs and traditions. Our history has demonstrated and serves today as an example that religion has not always loved itself.

Most religions that exist today are actually divided, and they should serve as proof that our institutions with their past religious leaders have failed to coexist with each other. It demonstrates how vulnerable our religious traditions are and how it can be changed by others that differ in their opinions. Factually, this is what has caused the division in different denominations of religion to increase, triggering our religions to continue branching itself into other spin-off religions with different traditions. Again, this should serve as further evidence how we as religious believers are very particular when it comes to our traditions or the way we believe. It should also serve as further proof of how many of us differ over interpretations of the same scriptures.

No one until Jesus could intellectually challenge the establishment with their knowledge about religion as He did. For others, this would result in death, as Jesus eventually suffered but later overcame. However, the way He was successful in His method to get this mob to focus on themselves as an example makes it possible for all of us to discover that there's much unknown to us about ourselves. It appears that we have a difficulty in accepting other people's values, especially if we already have established ourselves in belief of something else. Most of us will manipulate our way through religious facts presented to us in an effort not to be proven wrong. I believe that as a society we defend our choices of religion. When we choose to believe anything, we have the same attitude of not wanting to be wrong, and we will often defend things we don't fully understand.

The purpose of this chapter is to reveal the life and struggles of religious believers and to give readers an understanding for their challenges as well as an insight of the institutions that led them. The hope is to encourage others to examine themselves and their religious mandate more closely. Hopefully, it may encourage all of us to lead our future judgment of others by reflection on ourselves first. We will see that the God that we all seek is the one of love, and our love is a stronger motivational tool than our persuasion by condemnation of others. It's been said before that most religious people are the hardest to love and that their self-righteous treatment of others is partly responsible for this belief of them.

Understanding how to love religious believers of God is just as complicated as trying to understand all the religious traditions of mankind. Everyone is unique in their thinking as it relates to their religious beliefs and teaching of tradition. I think any of us considering any religious belief should consider that this needs to be done with some degree of caution, with the understanding that we can never be exactly sure of what someone is leading us to believe. I mean, every religion has divisions within itself anyway, and religion itself has a problem within its institution with all believing differently and divided because most differ in the interpretation of Scripture or philosophy.

Many who proclaim to know God struggle in relationships with each other, most of the time because of differences in belief. What I'm saying is that our religious leaders defend their position with others over their belief in their religion instead of leading most times through example. Most are robotic in their approach in dealing with foreign subjects that stretch their imagination as it relates to any new facts that are introduced to them about religions that differ from their beliefs. Many religious believers lack compassion, and they won't commit to mixing with those who differ from us. Actually, we will do this with people that claim to know God as well as those that don't. Religious believers tend to stay within their own elite club.

We are more divided now in religion than any other time in history, which is partly a result of all our evolving traditions and beliefs that continue to divide our religious society. It should serve as another example that our problem in religion is not that those who follow religion has not found a way to "love all," but rather that religion and its followers are learning how to love itself. This ongoing division within the institution of religion has confused leaders and believers alike in understanding how to love others as we love ourselves. It could be said that those who follow religion itself has not clearly led by example in demonstrating to others in how to actually "love thy neighbor as thyself." To me personally, this is another sign of the failure of mankind's way of traditions and the example of its imperfections.

I feel that if anyone seeks to look at mankind's religious traditions as their example of how to live, or if we believe that those that have fallen from grace as a reason for us not to believe in religion, then we need to recognize that this is an act classified by God as following mankind and is not led by our efforts to seek for ourselves. We are all very much human and vulnerable to do wrong. It's easier to find fault with people that are different from us, and so often the good qualities of others are overlooked, whether someone is religious or not. Normally, those that proclaim this belief are thought to be insensitive to others that have different traditions and beliefs, and their actions are often used as examples of how religion is flawed. I argue that the Word of God is not flawed—only that man has often failed in trying to live as the example of it.

Every religion or culture of religious believers seemingly births spin-offs of other traditions that are often more extreme or significantly different than before, with each competing for supremacy in its belief. Religion has demonstrated within its own belief system and with its diversified traditions that this will continue to conflict with itself, making all those who believe in God do so under great opposition with others as to who God is and how to please Him through our traditions. It appears to me that nonbelievers of religion as well as those who believe will better learn about religion and the religious traditions of men in two major ways.

One way this begins is when we understand that the responsibility is ours in gaining knowledge about God or religion. We must also believe that it's dangerous for anyone to expect any person on this earth to have a spiritual experience for us without our seeking God personally for ourselves, and we must realize that those that lead cannot always be a reliable source to follow.

Secondly, we must realize that most religions all refer to the same God. However, mankind's understanding of which God would depend on what tradition as well as what religion or culture. There can only be one solution to maximize our possibility for accuracy, and that can only come from our careful research of all related facts worthy of consideration.

It's not that this is necessarily a malicious intent aimed at religious believers. Rather, mankind's tradition for religion has evolved, and the way it has changed wasn't always the way God intended; it was established because mankind's interpretation of what some thought He wanted. Religion has a mandate for us to love all. Most gay and lesbian activists for equal rights would use this to support their cause, despite what some in religion may claim. I feel that those that are leaders and followers of our religion are facing uncharted territory in their need to answer many unchallenged questions in this complex subject that the world church faces today in learning how we all worship with and witness to those that are homosexual, as we do with others. It begins with us actually believing that we do not have the religious authority to treat someone different because we think we are closer to God. It is a mistake that others do using their self-prescribed authority to speak as if they are the Creator for religion when they do this.

Actually, I believe that homosexuality and religion do not conflict in the way we may think. Our division begins in how we avoid discussing this subject, although most religious believers are still likely to continue to judge everyone. I'm sure most religious people possess a sincere desire to be faithful in what they believe. We have leaned on our leaders for the understanding of complex matters of importance regarding how to understand God's written words. Ultimately, we are responsible for understanding the Almighty for ourselves. Our leaders are not necessarily responsible for us not having the desire to love God or forcing us to pursue a deeper relationship with Him. This is more than they can do for us.

I believe that our life lessons have taught us to verify people and to conduct an intensive investigation before we trust someone, and the same concept applies to us knowing God. When we research for knowledge about religion, it's actually an expression to God of our desire to seek Him. Jesus always tried to connect with those whom society rejected. He did this regardless of how religious believers of that day thought. He showed compassion for anyone who was in conflict with His teachings. Nevertheless, today it's more likely that we will ask others for their opinion about what God would want us to do or not do; however, the answer is only their opinion and not God's. We cannot allow others and their bad advice that's given to us to be reasons for our uneducated decisions. It's clear from history that mankind gets it wrong with its belief in religion over and over, and those that follow suffer.

In short, learning how to love religious people has its unique challenges. The responsibility of learning is ours, and the hunger to learn is created by our self-propelled desire to seek God more intimately.

6

Learning How to Love God

In our lives, there may be many reasons why learning how to love God can be difficult for us to obtain. Often, we may feel this big void inside of us, and we might know that we are an empty vessel needing to be filled. When other religious followers are trying to teach us about their religion, it can sometimes be more hurtful than helpful. It may seem that their lifestyles are so religious that they are too perfect for anyone to follow, making it difficult for most people to relate to them. We can be intimidated by people and how perfect they seem to us. As we are trying to learn about God from their prospective and the way they explain their relationship with their belief in religion, it can feel to us as if it is something impossible to do or much too difficult for us to obtain. We develop a kind of thinking that others may have a deeper grip of religion than we do.

As we attempt to follow our religious beliefs, we often use others as our examples to follow. Our lack of self-esteem influences us to compare ourselves to the way that we see others actually live and worship God. We feel as if there is no other way for us to verify our spiritual growth of whether we are on the same level as everyone else unless we understand what is normal or not with those associated with our religion. Sometimes we can change in our lives without realizing that we have adopted our new way of thinking from the influence of someone else. It would seem logical that if we are trying to learn about how to love God, we should begin by understanding how it has always been done in the past as well. This may later become the primary component that we will structure our morals and beliefs on. The fact is that when we're introduced to religions and all its traditions, our focus is usually on learning about the basics to form an opinion. We might try to study Scriptures for our knowledge or we might educate ourselves on ancient religion or other studies that will help us to learn more about God, but what we don't often learn is how to actually love God. Our concept of how to love a God that we haven't met has always been doubted by some and considered foolishness by others. Learning how to know God and finding what His commandments are for our lives is what is often taught by our religious leaders, and getting the knowledge of how to exactly love God is not always explained to us as clear as learning God's commandment for us.

It seems as if teaching others how to fear God has become more popular than the message of learning how to love Him. In fact, some teach of His judgment for mankind as if He is a Creator of vengeance or as if He is something that expects unreasonable expectations of us or as if God is more concerned with our obedience to Him. Although our religion makes it clear that His requirement is for us "to love our neighbors as we love ourselves," we are very seldom taught the importance of loving God. If we are taught that we should love Him, it really is not made clear to us how. Explaining that we should love something is different than explaining why we should and how we can. If we really examine the idea of loving a God we haven't met or probably will never meet in our physical bodies on this earth, then we must confess that it's a little hard for some to understand how that can be done. It always sounds pretty good to hear others claim that we should love Him. But is the love that we seek an actual love for God or is it out of God's commandment for us? Or is it out of fear for Him? I'm not sure that we've ever questioned these facts before or if we have ever questioned just how much we love Him and why. Although it's easier to clarify why we need to love God, it has been proven a little more difficult for most in finding how to love God.

Our concept of love could be confused with the romantic love that is more common, which is not the love that is meant with our Creator. Some of us may think of the concept of love from the different ways that they understand it. However, there is not a clear road map of what kind of a love relationship we should have with God, other than our loving Him as a priority above any other gods and knowing that He is supreme in our concept of who is responsible for our creation. However, that doesn't really define what kind of love we should have for Him exactly. One of the ways for us to understand what is expected for us is that we must consider the scriptures that imply how mankind should love God ("with all of our mind and all of our heart"), and when we do this, we will understand more what kind of love God meant. Discovering how to love God can be just as much of a challenge as trying to understand how and why God has such love for us. Doing this challenges us to take inventory of ourselves and our level of love for God.

For some people learning how to love God can be difficult because of the guilt that we carry. Often, we carry so much guilt in our lives because we are not perfect, and we definitely have not lived perfect lives. The memory of things that we have previously done may play in our head as if it is on auto-start when we think about God. It's as if our guilt tries to remain in control of us. Our guilt has led us to feel that we are not worthy of God like others are, and even though we may hear preachers say that we are forgiven, it may still feel to us as if that message was somehow meant for others.

Those learning how to love God with guilt can feel as if they owe God a debt that can never be paid. We can literally feel overwhelmed from our past, despite what others tell us. In order for some of us to believe God, many may wish that He would come down and personally deliver His message of forgiveness to us. Everyone's reasons for the need of learning may differ from others, but the struggle and experiences that are felt are all similar. Some of our struggles can be because of losing someone that we love, and seemingly to some, God is responsible for our troubles. Or it could be that we think we have lived right and followed all the rules of life of loving everyone and living honestly, yet your life has been disastrous. Whatever our reasons are, we have somehow decided that God is not fair. In fact, sometimes we might go as far as to curse Him for the pain that life has caused us. We blame Him for the bad things in our life because He is the Creator of this world, and we feel that He's the one responsible for the disasters in the world.

For some of us, God has never shown Himself at all, not even in the slightest way. We may be confused as to how others obtain this Holy Ghost type of experience. This can make someone seeking God really feel as if they're missing out on something that God is giving to others. We might have heard of some people who even claim that their bodies have been healed or how others have faced supernatural out-of-body experiences after they died and came back to life. All this can make us feel that God somehow cares for others, but not us. For some of us, trying to understand why God loves others and not us is how we may begin to feel and think continuously. Often, we may feel as if we are cursed by God because of all the things that continue to go wrong in our lives, and trying to learn how to love God for these individuals may take time. As we heal over time, we are able to see God differently. Our pain and sorrow that we feel soon becomes replaced with the awareness of how unmanageable our lives are without God, and with our continued efforts, our lives eventually become manageable for us again.

Although trying to learn to love God will remain difficult as some will continue to blame Him. It is possible for us to become like the children of Israel, where Moses parted the Red Sea that made their freedom possible. The Bible states that because of their lack of faith in God, they were lost in the desert for forty years. They continued to blame God and Moses after he parted the Red Sea and they obtained their freedom, and because they were lost after time most no longer had trust in God. The Bible declares that without any of us having faith in God, it is impossible to please Him. Therefore, as we all seek to know how to love God, we must first learn to trust Him; and most often, this is when most of us fail. Our inability to let go of our worries of what will happen to us as we are trying to surrender all of it to God is what's hard for most. We might say we love God and that we're willing to follow his commandments, but for us to actually let go of our worries, most of us will not trust God that far. We probably never thought that this is God's way of measuring our love for Him through our demonstration of the way that we trust Him. Or maybe God considers that to be an act of our faith.

The way God feels is similar to our experiences if someone we love will not trust us. We would be offended, especially if we have already given our best efforts to prove our love to them. God feels this same way. He really does require our relationship with Him to be compared to how we love others. In doing so, we might eventually better understand God and why He could be a jealous God with His love for us, just as we are with our love for others. As I'm thinking of God this way, it gives more clarification as to why our having faith is so essential and better explains what faith is. Once we do better understand that our relationship with God is similar to what we expect of others, we can then better expect what God might feel as a result of what we say and do. We really don't know that when we do believe, it is an act essentially telling God that we have faith in Him, as we sometimes may say we do. God feels the same. It is said in Scripture that "we are made in the image of God." This would indicate the type of emotions we feel that He also feels, and without our faith in Him, God is declaring that we cannot please Him.

Most religious leaders and followers of God all struggle with having enough faith in God. It's a rare attribute for most to acquire and maintain, and it requires us to let go of our worries of life, knowing that God will protect us. However, part of learning how to have faith in God is when we are able to remember the many times that God has been active in our lives and the many ways He has protected us and those we love. Through our experiences with God over time, we began to love Him because of His faithfulness to us. Most of us think of faith in God as just trusting God, but only partly is it trusting him. Although, it is a similar process of how we all began to love anyone, and it usually starts first with trust, is followed by faith, and eventually turns into love. In learning how to love God through faith, we must put the pieces of all our experiences together to totally begin to see how God was still working in our lives when we were unaware of it. Once our storms of life have passed and things have become clearer, we will gradually heal spiritually and emotionally.

Learning how to love God after we have experienced life's disasters can be what gives us more reason to seek God or, for others, more of a reason to doubt that He was ever there for us. There are others that may have actually been victimized by someone claiming to represent God. These individuals have often been misled while just beginning to know who He is. Now those claiming to know God may all be just like the person who victimized them, and when religion is mentioned, it can stir up their emotions. Some of us can actually respond negatively to others about the subject of religion as a result of how we feel inside. There are those individuals which at one time were learning how to love God, but they now are recovering from the leadership of those who were not authentic and honest and had fallen from grace. Trying to recover from those that have done this is not easy and could definitely be considered a challenge for those learning how to love God. Most people will use this as proof that religion is flawed, and it is because of this that many don't recover. Learning how to love God after we have been let down *before* by religious leaders can be an uphill battle and difficult to overcome. I did personally experience this with my dad, who was a minister as well as with other religious leaders who I had sought for spiritual guidance. Although what they taught me about God was not misleading, it was how they lived that bothered me.

Although trying to learn how to love God can be difficult when we have been deceived before by our spiritual leaders and mentors, it can motivate us to pursue things about our religion with caution in the future. The advantage of going through this is that we start independently thinking for ourselves instead of being actually led by others. In my previous experiences with my dad and other ministers, instead of praying by myself, I actually used their prayer with God as if it was my very own. As a consequence of any of us doing this, we do not exercise our spiritual muscles. They become weak because we allow our leaders and mentors to think and feel for us, and we fail to depend on our own communication with God.

Learning how to love God after having a failed experienced leadership may require some rehabilitation, and our recovery from this actually depends on how much of our trust was put on our leaders or on God. I fundamentally had a strong foundation of belief for God. However, at that time, I had wondered if anyone was capable or honest enough to follow their belief, as they claimed. I became unsure as to whether it is possible for someone to be committed to religion, as they say. This is a result of having seen many leaders fall, and many other followers live their lives contrary to what they say they believe. I started to question if all our leaders of religion and those that follow it are actually being sincere about their belief in God. It took a deep desire for me to really want to know God better—not just a desire to know Him but a deeper desire not to fail Him, as I had seen with others. I feel that if anyone has ever personally witnessed the fall of a religious leader, only then would we better understand why this is a situation nobody would want to experience for themselves.

Despite this, it can be a sobering spiritual experience that allows us to open our eyes more widely to what we are being taught and who we are putting our faith in. The experience of seeing others fall from grace could be used as our excuse for not believing in those who claim religion, or we can use this as a way to get our strength and courage to overcome the dark forces that will lure us away from the reality of religion. I feel that the difference is our having an attitude in the beginning, which dictates this and a desire of not failing God as others before us.

Learning how to love God can seem to be impossible to us if we have lived a controversial lifestyle that everyone around us knows and will always remember. Feeling this way takes special spiritual courage because there are always others that will remind us of our past, as if it is their self-designated duty for God. Often, these can be the very religious people that we expect to be there to support us. Deep inside, we may feel that we are not on their level. It may seem to us that no matter what we accomplish, it will never be good enough to rise up to a level like others around us. We might feel that maybe God may have forgotten our past lifestyles, but the people that knew us before will not.

Learning how to love God around those who refuse to forget our past is difficult, even if others are trying to support us. It can be hard for us to look someone square in the eyes with a feeling of confidence that we are equal to them. It is as if we feel that we owe a debt that has not been paid to God. For some people, learning how to love God is difficult because no one has ever presented anything about religion or God to them. Most of these individuals have no concept of where to begin in their search to understand this subject. They lack exposure to know what God considers good or bad by not having the needed skills other than the common things taught to them. These individuals can be easily influenced by the predators of false religions, and they can fall trap to incorrect concepts of who God is. Often, most don't have the tools to verify facts about who God is or what He requires of us. Most people will learn of religion from others and their perspective, and they will ultimately form an opinion of everything about religion based upon these total experiences.

There are those learning how to love God again, after having already failed him. There can be many reasons why someone would feel that they have failed God. Actually, there are fallen religious leaders that are learning how to love God all over again. Although I'm not a fallen leader, I feel that I can still relate because I'm a fallen follower of God. I have fallen enough to understand how it feels to disappoint God and myself and others. We can feel as though we've committed the ultimate offense against God. When we're learning how to love God all over again is because we've discovered that in our first attempt to do this that we've failed and dishonored ourselves, and most times some that do this have taught people to know who God is for years, and now they might feel that they are the ultimate hypocrite of what they have always represented to others.

Learning how to love God again for those that feel they have failed God may remind some of Judas who had forsaken Jesus. It can be hard for us to accept God's forgiveness, even if we get on the right track again. We will always question whether we will be capable to sustain it. We will always fear that we can never rise to the level that we were before with God. These individuals who are learning how to love God again live with guilt for what they have done against God, despite his forgiveness. We still struggle with the knowledge of what we have done, and our minds will forever battle us in our attempt to forgive ourselves.

Learning how to love God after we have failed Him before can give us a feeling of inferiority when we are trying to speak about the subject. In fact, it can be more difficult to accomplish than we might imagine. Attempting to get over the feeling that we have let Him down before makes us feel as if we no longer have that authority to speak on the subject of religion again. Then there are those who are learning how to love God because of the forced influence of someone else. This usually happens when someone has good intentions to help us, but they require us to follow their way of religion in order to satisfy them. In this situation, we are usually not in power of making decisions, or at least it may feel that way when we do this. Whether it's our mate, a relative, or a friend, we find ourselves committed to someone for what they have done for us. We often feel pressured to act as if we actually enjoy what is going on. It's not as if we don't appreciate others' help; it's more that learning how to love God the way others think we should is not what motivates us. In fact, feeling as if we have to do something without a choice is sometimes counterproductive in the results that we all we seek.

Learning how to love God without it being our choice or a feeling that we have to satisfy someone else can lead to our confusion. Instead of us satisfying God, we are actually satisfying someone else's expectations, and our reason for following is often only because we expect something from them and not from God. Often, our circumstances will dominate our attention, and our focus on God will be more of a show for others than reflecting on how we actually feel. Learning how to love God while we are trying to impress someone else about our religious commitment can lead us to getting our knowledge of God with the wrong intentions, and it may also lead us to a false understanding of our Creator and become a barrier in our attempt to actually find Him.

There are those who are learning how to love God, and trying to learn means they must risk their lives. I know it may seem impossible to imagine that this still exists in our world today, but the process of learning for these individuals is dark and scary. There are things other people around the world enjoy without thought, but they often have not considered that others have risked and sometimes given their lives just so they could have what we totally take for granted. I often imagine how scary it could be learning how to love God this way. In order to understand who God is for them, they literally have to risk their lives for something that they spiritually believe. Just this thought alone would keep most from seeking God out of fear of religious persecution, and the process of learning how to love God would never get started. It's almost as if it was somehow designed to be snuffed out before the education about God and religion and love for others begins to bloom with anyone. I have not experienced this type of cruelty as others have. I can only imagine the type of courage it takes in trying to worship God under such circumstances. I cannot say with certainty that I could be as courageous as those who are willing to die purposely while taking such a chance to defend their pursuit to worship God and their religion. Most people in this world have not had to experience this in their lives. It seems that we do not have the appropriate appreciation for our religious freedom as we should.

There are also those that are learning how to love God that are in bondage somewhere in the world, locked away in prison from the reality that we take for granted. Some might argue that these individuals deserve what they get, but in the eyes of God, they are no different than all others that seek God. These individuals seek to learn how to love God under probably the worst living conditions on earth. Their justification for religion will be thought by most to be something temporary until they are released or maybe a way to cope while they're doing time. When these individuals seek to learn how to love God, they first must learn to love themselves. This can be particularly difficult for someone incarcerated, who some believe is not deserving of the air we breathe. These individuals rise from the feeling of hopelessness to the possibility that God will love and forgive them, even though the world will not. Those that are incarcerated often face confinement alone for days and nights, and they continuously use their imagination to imitate our natural world. It must be horrifying to live this way while learning how to love God, but for those that do, the belief of God and faith can be their only lifeline to sanity. They feel that they are forgotten from the world, and they question if God even knows that they still exist. Their feeling of abandonment is a feeling that allows me to know that what they endure is relevant, and it gives justification as to why we should consider the lives of others that are in prison with the same consideration we give to ours. It could be said that those incarcerated have nothing left in life to look forward to, and that is why they are just now turning to religion. Although I don't personally think that it matters what inmates' reasons are for seeking God in their time of need, being that it is available for all of us when we finally decide that we are ready to accept.

The fact is that everyone has a story that is important, and others benefit when we are able to share that experience. Often there are leaders and followers of religion that think they are closer to religion because of their belief and position of authority, and they treat others selectively. Sometimes learning how to love God with this type of leadership can make you feel like you have had a bad religious experience. While most of our leaders are worthy of praise, there are those who will intimidate others and sometimes will downright send people to hell before you can say, "I'm sorry" for whatever you said or done. It seems that there are some people that exist just to make people feel that God will never love us. They act as if God is exclusive to them and as if we should be privileged to share their time and hear their stories of success. In fact, the feeling that most of us can get from how great these leaders are can intimidate any amateur believer of God into questioning their worthiness or faith.

It seems that as we are trying to learn about God, we sometimes meet others who seem to have more knowledge about religion than we do. These people can be classified as "books in walking shoes." They will know everything about God. These certain individuals will seemingly confess to know us and our future as well as what to expect that God has for our family. They will give us a false knowledge of religion, and their motivation should always be questionable. These types of individuals that I'm trying to describe are what I consider as being professional religious con artists. In this situation, trying to learn how to love God can be tricky. These individuals come as wolves in sheep clothing. They are equipped with a silver tongue that is designed to manipulate others. There are many today suffering from their wounds that were inflicted by these types of con artists of religion. If you have become a victim of someone like this after being led by a false leadership, learning how to love God will be different than before. As we attempt to be "normal" again in our religion, after already being led wrongly by someone else before, this could give us a feeling of distrust of what we've been taught or a reason to doubt the things told to us again in the future.

Okay, the first question by some could be, is God and religion the same thing? How can I love something that I haven't seen? These are fundamental questions that actually all those that know religion personally should have the ability to answer. If not, that's still okay because religion is established with God as its centerpiece and foundation, but there still is a difference between the two.

God is love and is an actual living spirit that also communicates with our spirit and coexists within our soul. Religion is a tradition of man. It is mankind's established way of showing our love, praise, and commitment to God. When religion acts out its judgment upon the world, most times God is held responsible as a result of mankind's traditions that were meant to honor God. What we actually do to change others sometimes have the opposite intended effect. Understanding that God is not directly responsible for how man maneuvers religion on his behalf should give healing to some that may have blamed him for religious acts of men. It also should help us to realize that the name of God actually means "love," and understanding this concept would lead us to all conclude that it's almost impossible to hate love.

In other words, to hate God is to hate the entire concept of love. Therefore, concluding that we all love "to be loved," which means we all love God. It's kind of simple, this way of knowing God. I believe being capable of understanding Him was designed by God to be simple to understand, and its mankind's religion that has confused this concept of God.

Mankind has taken the interpretation of God and over time has manipulated his Word to fit man's tradition in religion. Actually, it's gotten so bad over time that religions have divided themselves into thousands of denominations that have different religious traditions. There was this explosion of spin-off beliefs that most fought to death to establish. Many of our religious beliefs all share one thing in common, and that is they all believe in a God and were willing to defend their principle.

History gives us the advantage today to examine and analyze those who lived before us. This ability to examine the history of man's relationship with God and its religious traditions are tools that should be used by those in our society today as an example of what we should and should not do. One of the first noticeable things from our violent religious history that I've noticed is the fact that these religious wars represent examples of how things happen that was not intended most times by God.

The division of different religions is a reflection of the lack of love and respect that religious leaders have shown for each other over time. Of course, this has not changed. Even today, there will be members of some religions that one day might branch off to form their own congregation of believers. This is a consequence of a shakeup in relationships among church members. The shakeup amongst religious members commonly started from unsettled disagreements, which in general could be considered lack of love and respect for each other.

In most cases, these are leaders and members that should possess the ability to teach this concept of love to others. However, history proves differently, and those who seek and claim to know

God, sometimes in their attempt to teach this belief their way, only highlight their lack of ability to lead. Their religious views will be seen by history as being opposite to what God expects of us. Now that we are able to see through the eyes of the past, we are able to better understand from this that some religious believers defend their point with violence. To them, their justification generally is to overcome others with the power of their gods.

It is therefore safe to say this: Coming together with other religious believers would have been a super challenge for us. I'm sure some would argue that point. But it's clear to me that there are many different spinoff religions that once began as one. This can serve as proof of that lack of love and respect that I'm using as an example. Religion is an illustration of man's attempt to honor their God of love, but it also highlights man's failure in its attempt to be an example of love.

We have proven to be much better at teaching and preaching than we are at showing true love for those that we attempt to teach and preach to. In fact, it appears that mankind has mastered this technique of religion. Most have mastered the technique of telling us of our godly failures and responsibilities. They have also mastered the technique of marketing their message to the world to grow their ministry, but the substance of the message of love and God have often proven to not be the centerpiece of their values of life. I would not expect for any religious institution that has a problem loving each other within its institution to be experts at teaching others this message of love. Nevertheless, it does highlight a much bigger point, and that is: if all people, religious or nonreligious, could examine ourselves first by asking the question, "Do we know God, and who is God?" By doing so, we can begin to answer the fundamental question that is necessary to understand who God is because it's true. How can you love something that you don't know? Nonetheless, as stated before, God is love, and we can all relate to what love is. If we let our minds focus on this point and mediate on this concept of love for others, we are actually entertaining our minds with that of God. Loving anyone is demonstrating that we have a part of God within us. To know God requires our effort to seek Him. If we let someone else do this research for us, we actually would be doing so at great risk of failure. It's hard to miss those that possess the spirit of God because the love they have is obvious and contagious.

7

Learning How to Love Gays

In learning how to love gays, I must admit that in my past, I am guilty of my condemnation of homosexuals. For me, it all started as an innocent joke. I didn't know anything about homosexuality before this. Starting at the age of twelve, the type of guys I hung out with over time molded my mind about homosexuality. Most of these guys were not religious and had a hard exterior look. I mean these were street guys, the kind that you would see hanging on a corner or at a liquor store. At that time, I totally had no idea what the word *homosexuality* was or what it meant. I had recently moved from a small town in Colorado to the city of San Diego, California. These guys were definitely different than the friends that I had normally hung out with.

My journey in discovering what homosexuality was all started while my friends and I were hanging out together riding the transit system around the city of San Diego, while looking to have fun. When doing so, we often encountered homosexual men who became the target of our harassment while riding the bus. This was the moment that I would learn several new words of our language, such as faggot, homo, etc. At that time, I did not know how anyone thought of homosexuality because I didn't know what it was. No one had ever discussed anything remotely close to what homosexuals or gay and lesbians were. Seeing my friends taunt homosexuals that we saw every day began to influence me eventually into doing the same. But I must admit that it did leave a bad feeling each time after I did this. Some of the homosexuals that we started taunting were the men that were fully loaded as a woman. Of course, at that time, it took a lot of efforts by others around me to convince me that they were not making a mistake claiming that these females were male. They had me fooled, but the guys with me knew better. They would later tell me the various ways that I could tell if they were a man or woman.

The beginning of my summer vacation in San Diego is when I started hanging out with these guys. I had never caught the bus before this as they did. They would ride all over San Diego and transfer to different buses after hanging out in different places of the city. There was no other place around town that had more action than downtown. At that time, there was a central bus stop downtown called "The Plaza" where everyone would transfer to different buses that went in different directions over the whole city. This was a central hub for the city, and it brought all different classes of people together. This is where you would find many street people. There were winos and drunkards that lived in the streets as well as the religious picketers displaying warning signs of the impending end of the world. There were hippies and Hare Krishna people beating their tambourines and dancing around the plaza. There were also the hustlers, pimps, prostitutes, and transvestites. My friends began to explain to me how some of these prostitutes that looked like ladies were actually men.

As my friends and I walked the streets of downtown San Diego and when we saw homosexual people, that was when we began our mischief. Most of the time, we would say funny jokes about them with each other and laugh or say something vulgar. After we would say that to them, we would all run away. I did not really think twice about what we were doing because we did it to just about everyone that looked out of the ordinary to us. For me, that entire experience was all about enjoying the summer fun, hanging out with friends all day, and seeing parts of the city that I had never seen before. Although we were pretty evil to others that we came in contact with, we never hurt anyone or were ever physical; it was all verbal abuse mixed with laughter. I would later begin to wonder how these homosexual men dressed like women were able to prostitute themselves. I couldn't understand how they could trick a man into thinking they were a woman.

At that time, my understanding of homosexuality was limited to men. I did not know that women could be this way too. Of course, I would later find out more about women, but at that time, I was too busy having summer fun with a bunch of friends that I had just met. We would meet up practically every day on the bus. Most of the time, we would meet downtown as all buses that everyone transferred to would go there. It was the best spot for all of us to meet because most of us lived in different neighborhoods of San Diego. I later found out that some of these friends had actually done time in a juvenile prison. Over time, they would share their experiences with me of what they went through while being locked up. This is when I learned how these guys developed their hatred for homosexuals. Of course, for them their word of preference for describing homosexuals was the word "faggot," and at that time, it seemed to me that they had deep knowledge about homosexuals. They would tell me about their experiences with homosexuals while being in juvenile detention with them. It was clear from what they were telling me that if a male homosexual was in jail at that time, it would have been very dangerous for them. They told me also that if anyone was caught smoking a cigarette after them that they were smoking, or if someone would touch a homosexual's hands or their mouth with their mouth, no one would ever share a cigarette with that person ever again. If someone did do that, they would be considered by others as being contaminated. What I did not understand was how some inmates would engage in sex and later would continue to treat them as if they were contaminated. It did not seem that it would be consistent with their ideas about sharing cigarettes.

My friend's knowledge about his juvenile detention experience with homosexuals began to become a source of information that I started believing about all homosexuals. Although I was still confused, I could not understand why there are those inmates that say they hate homosexuals but will have sex with gays and afterward don't consider themselves to be homosexuals; they'd say they were just satisfying themselves because there were no women around.

Learning to understand the way others thought became to be important to me. I really didn't understand all his jail stories of how all this was possible. This subject was just as different as it was hanging out with them over the summer. It seemed that his story went together with my whole adventure of hanging with them as a juvenile in the streets. They were both new and different facts of learning about life. What I learned from that summer about how others felt about homosexuality and their many reasons for their hatred of others that were gay somehow became a part of the way I thought for years. When I first found out about homosexuality, it seemed that my religious tradition was somehow never an issue with me, and it was not even considered. I never thought homosexuality would one day be a part of my own family as well. I was mixed up in my thinking about homosexuality; in fact, I thought of it as nothing but different things that the world does that I am just learning about. I thought more in terms of sexual relationships, not personal relationships. I must admit that back then, my desire was not to become friends with homosexuals because of the things I had learned over that summer. I carried those thoughts for years, although I had no hatred of homosexuals. It was more that this reaction to gays was the only way I had ever learned to react to them. It was as if I had the privilege to disrespect them because I always got away with it without getting in trouble. I felt that when my friends and I did this together, it somehow justified my reasoning for the way we treated homosexuals.

The fact is that as I got older, my views evolved about homosexuality. I no longer thought that it was okay to act so stupid in how I treated others that were gay. Besides, I thought, one of my juvenile friends nearly got beat up in downtown San Diego by someone we were making fun of. We all were chased for several blocks by this masculine 240 pound man with a deep voice who was dressed as a woman. It later seemed to me as something that can be hazardous to my health, if I continued doing it. After that event, I better understood that these ladies were actually men, and sometimes they could be stronger and tougher than most men. I always remembered that day as a way to remind me of how doing this can turn out to be a dangerous and unpleasant experience. For me, this experience helped to change me from acting childish as I did before. But I still had feelings that homosexuals were not equal to everyone else. It seemed to me that my justification for feeling that way was that everyone I knew thought that it was a more socially acceptable way of dealing with homosexuality, and there was no one really defending homosexuality and their rights at that time. There was no one I could communicate with to get any information on the subject of homosexuality at that time. It also seemed to me that any information that I did learn about the subject was always negative. It was considered a lifestyle that no one felt comfortable in discussing.

After I started high school, everything about other people's homosexuality seemed to become clearer. At school, some of those students actually chose to expose their sexuality to everyone without fear for the first time. There were women and men whose sexual preferences were now noticeable to me unlike before. Of course, I knew that I no longer could treat them as I had treated other homosexuals before with my friends. This time, I was unaffected by their presence. I noticed who and what they were, but I had no opinion that affected my feelings as before. Throughout my high school years, my knowledge about homosexuality did not really increase; in fact, my passion for sports, cars, dancing, girls, and hanging out with friends was all I really thought about. I never tried to analyze the subject as I had done years before. I simply looked at others that were dressed the opposite of their sex to be their way of a sexual expression to others. *It was nothing more than just sex acts that they do*, I thought. My opinion was formed from the lack of education on this subject. I was trying to understand something that I really did not care about. At the time, I did not know anyone who was homosexual, so it meant nothing to me.

Although I attended church two to three times every week, I never remember anyone talking about the subject of homosexuality there as well. All the religious followers and leaders throughout my life have never spoken much, if any, about homosexuality. It seems to me that if you are not a homosexual, trying to learn about this subject can be more challenging than we might imagine, and it should serve as proof that most others must judge homosexuality in the very same inexperienced way as I did. Now it's clear that there are leaders and followers of religion that have always condemned homosexuality. As I've gotten older, I have now witnessed that, but at that time it seemed that nobody really discussed the subject.

Nevertheless as I continued high school and sports, I began to bond with other athletes who were homosexuals—mostly female track runners and a male cheerleader. With this friendly relationship that was limited to the playing field, I started feeling as though it was weird and different. However, most of the homosexuals were friendlier and more compassionate than others appeared to be. I was either excited about their athletic performance on the playing field, or they shared in my success on the track field. When you're winning, no one really cares about who everyone is. Often when you're celebrating and enjoying the spirit of your teammates. From this, it seemed that having something in common is how teammates in all sports are able to bond. I made friends with some of the homosexual athletes that were also my high school teammates, and when I left school, I felt as if I had also left my school friends there. I had totally different friends after school. I was part of a car club, and we hung out together on the weekends. How I socialized with teammates versus my other friends was different. I felt closer to them than my friends at my school. These friends in the streets were antigay and hardcore, and they were the type of guys that would start accusing me of being gay if they knew I had gay friends. I never felt comfortable with my street friends in admitting to them that I had friends at school that were homosexual. However, I did feel more comfortable around the female athletes who were gay; for me, they posed no potential harm to my reputation.

The male athletes or students who I knew were gay, I treated with short but respectful conversations. However, when I spoke to *men* that were homosexuals, I must have appeared to be nervous to them because I would always look around first to see who was looking before speaking to them. As I was talking to them, I would always continue looking to see who was watching as we talked. I feel bad about the way I was, but I was terrified of anyone thinking that I might be like they were. I at least wanted to be polite to others, but I knew that some of my street friends would consider that questionable. They felt that if anyone talks to a gay person, they must be one also. At least that was how I felt others would think, and I really was afraid of getting put in that situation with them or anyone else. I suppose most of my street friends had formed their opinions about homosexuals while they were in jail, and all my school friends had never seen a jail; most were just forming their opinions about homosexuality. Because of that, I felt as though those at my school were really not up-to-date with the streets and everything that was going on out there as my street friends were. I suppose had I not hung around my streets friends during that summer, I would not know any more about homosexuality than some of my school friends that were still learning.

I graduated in the year 1976, and at that time, it seemed as if homosexuality just suddenly began to be more popular. There was an explosion of people everywhere expressing their homosexuality. Everyone that was against it was angry, and no one could find a solution for their anger or a way to deal with it. But that was also a time in which our country was changing dramatically and was faced with change with "civil rights," "women's rights," "abortion rights" and many other social inequalities. It seemed that everyone's rights in our society were on fire to promote change. Of course, as I said before, I really did not care about anything that was happening outside of my world.

It seems that my street friends had learned to hate homosexuals, and I was beginning to learn from them. I suppose what I'm saying is that we must be taught to hate others. It is hard to hate someone that you don't know anything about. Maybe I knew that it was weird when I first saw a man dressed as a woman, but I did not understand what it was all about to form an opinion. The opinions that I formed independent of my friends was simply an innocent nonbiased way of analyzing them because I knew nothing about homosexuality—only that this guy was dressed as a woman and I was trying to understand *why* they were dressed that way without anyone else's influence to get me to hate them. After being around my friends, that was when the pieces of the unsolved puzzles of homosexuality began to come together for me. That was when I started understanding from them that it was something bad. Before this, I knew that it was an unusual thing for a man to do, but I never thought of it as being bad until someone said that it was. My point is only how we are so influenced by our environment, that the decisions we make are not because of our efforts of researching the facts that are suggested to us by others.

As I grew older, my opinions about homosexuality did evolve, and it evolved not just because of things that were told to me by others. Now I was actually making my independent decisions based on my views from life's experiences. One of these experiences came when my friend and I were cruising around the city in his fancy car. His car was money-green with a money sign on each side of his car. He wanted to be the best in fashion, money, and cars. He drove around until he came to a hotel. He told me to wait outside while he met with a lady inside; it wasn't long before he came back. He was sweating and breathing rapidly as he began to turn the key to his ignition. He said to me, "That lady was a man!" I didn't dare ask him what he had done. However, he had admitted to having kissed, so I immediately started throwing up my old defenses learned from my other group of friends. Now I was thinking, *He is now contaminated!* I quickly asked myself, *Should I smoke behind my friend after he's done that?* I laughed at first. It was real funny, and it still is to me now, but he did not take it well. He was really upset and begged me not to tell our friends. He never told me not to ever write about it though. Sadly, he passed away about three years later after I graduated high school and after I got married. He drowned swimming somewhere in Tijuana, Mexico, with his friends near Baja, California. This homosexual experience that my friend had gone through came as further education for me regarding knowledge of homosexuality. Actually, this made me begin to question whether females were actually females in those that I met for years to come. In fact, I had questioned females sometimes to the extreme that some had to show me their proof before I could be certain that they were 100 percent female.

Shortly after this happened to him, I felt that if other friends of mine had found out what he did, they would think he's contaminated and would question why he and I were hanging out together. I felt now that I was becoming an expert on homosexuals and how to know if women were really women or men. I thought that there were several things about their bodies that would give it away. Some would say, "Look at their "\Adam's apple," while others would say, "You can tell from their bone structure." Then there's some that think you can tell better by the sound of their voice or the way they walk. I feel that the facial bone structure can sometimes be revealing, but generally, a man's feet will always give it away for most. Examining people was the beginning of scientific interest to me, and not just homosexuals. Going downtown, you would have a selection of many different people to talk to or analyze by just watching. I began to make it a part-time habit to watch others. I think the need to see if ladies were really men or not started in me as a quest to analyze others that I could not reverse such as looking at women to see if they were men or the need to question men's or women's real sexual identity. I know that we might consider that stereotyping, but I thought what I was doing to be a more fair way of stereotyping others, mainly because I felt that some homosexuals were unfair by not revealing to others that they were actually men. This was my way of getting my protection from that threat.

I started noticing when the men I saw everyday had one or two earrings in their ear or when they would wear bright colors. At that time, it was a sign that men were homosexual if they wore two earrings or bright colors. I would start to think that any man that was a little feminine must be a homosexual. I also thought if someone bends their wrist downward as they are talking or if they swung their hips from side to side while walking, then they must also be gay. I began to feel that I was an authority on this subject, and I wanted to continuously learn more about others and their different secret things that they don't reveal.

It seems that just as I was getting the idea that I knew everything about homosexuals and how it worked, I had to deal with finding out that one of my four sisters was a homosexual. It was later after I graduated from high school, and shortly after I was married. My wife and I were at a park just enjoying the day when something took place that led to us talking about homosexuality. My wife and I had recently seen love letters in my sister's car that were addressed to my sister from her girlfriend. As we were discussing the subject on homosexuality, my wife once again told me that my sister was gay. When she told me that, I cursed at her and called her a liar. I was full of rage because I thought that she was lying to me. This started to renew my hatred for homosexuals, but then I suddenly realized that now I would have to add my sister to the list of all the gays that I thought were contaminated. The fact is, I did not think that I could feel the same for her as I used to for others that were homosexuals. I felt angry, but I did not know who to be angry at. Although I was very angry at hearing about my sister, I don't recall ever asking her about whether it was true or not. I believe that it actually verified what I had seen in her at home as kids, but I did not pay any attention until now. Even though I was angry at my sister, I was too afraid to ask her if she was gay. I'm not sure if I was angry or if it was just my ego that had been affected.

I had stopped hanging out with some of my street friends that rode the bus by now—mainly because I had found a car— but what I learned from them about homosexuality was really bothering me. I did not want to feel that sort of hatred toward my sisters, as I always did with other homosexuals. Also, I did not want to think that this was actually happening to me and my family. In fact, I wanted to think that somehow it was a temporary incident or phase that was going on and that maybe they were just both exploring their sexuality and they would go back to being "normal." But again, all the evidence I had been ignoring was always there in front of me and I failed to catch it. I was actually not a good judgment of character of people as I thought I was. *How could I have missed this?* I thought over and over again. I knew one of my sisters was always sort of like a tomboy, but I never thought much about it. *When they are your younger sisters, we don't notice everything*, I thought. I was now feeling guilty for not paying more attention to my sisters as I could have, and actually in some small way, I was making myself responsible for their homosexuality choice as well. I thought that I was taking this harder than others in my family. I felt I had spent more time with my sisters than any other sibling of mine, and perhaps that is why I am more passionate about their being a homosexual.

It was good timing that I was married when I found out that two of my sisters were gay. I had someone to give support to me and help keep my emotions from overwhelming me. My wife also provided different female perspectives about the way they may think and feel, things that I had not considered before this. I used my wife as a partial way to relate to my sisters. It seemed as if I had no idea what females were and how they thought at that time. If I don't know who my sisters really are after living with them for so long, how can I be certain of anything? After I got married, I did not see much of my sisters at all. I worked two jobs and went to college and came home to help raise our children. The time with my sisters that I took daily for granted was now becoming memories. I had no idea what they were doing in their lives for years after that. Both my sisters and their female partners had been married for several years, and presently, they are still together. After we all became involved with someone, we become private in our immediate families, or maybe it was just me or something else led to me being so ignorant about what they were doing in their lives.

After time, I discovered that I had other relatives that were homosexual. It had been obvious to everyone else in Colorado except my immediate family because these cousins lived in another state and were not raised around us. I've met the family on several occasions throughout the years, but not enough to consider myself close to my cousin. However, we were all very young when I first saw my cousin. I may have been six years old, and I possibly saw him two to three times between six years to eighteen years old. It was exciting being able to see relatives again after so long. My cousin's name was Jimmy. I met him again after moving back to Colorado from California. Although I had several other cousins in Colorado, Jimmy was the only one that everyone seemed to know was homosexual. He lived with his male friend, and I had a chance to meet them both when I went to visit him on two occasions. I did not feel any of the typical feelings that I got around other homosexuals. With Jimmy, his strong personality and loud voice could light up a crowded room. He always had a smile and was full of energy. He loved loud music and dancing. When I visited him, I brought my wife and family with me, and we treated him as we would anyone else. It felt strange seeing him and his boyfriend share the same home, but it did seem clean and cozy. He presented himself to be the same ole Jimmy I always knew. He was cracking jokes and talking about Hollywood stars, music, and gossip about famous people. He talked also about his home, his passion for living there, and caring for his home. I didn't visit long, but in the short time I was there, we talked enough to catch up on things we missed through the years.

After leaving his house for the first time, I felt that I now know homosexuals on a more personal level than before. It was my first time ever being in a home that two men shared together as a couple. I felt that I was turning my back on my former way of thinking. I felt that somehow I was slowly becoming to accept this lifestyle. I know that it was just a visit to a cousin that I cared for, but somehow, it felt as if it was more than that to me. However, on my second visit, I took additional time to visit by watching the Broncos game with him and his partner. In that visit, I was able to relax more, and I enjoyed my visit with him better. I did not know that this would be one of my last visits with Jimmy, as I later found out that he and his partner were dying from AIDS. It was a devastating time for my aunt and her other children. They all came together before his death; even his job advanced him monies to buy a Cadillac. Jimmy spent his last time with me when my wife and I gave him a BBQ party at our house and we rode in his Cadillac that I helped him find. He purchased the car that he had always dreamed about, and I saw the joy in him as he turned up his music and danced in his seat as he drove. Those last days with Jimmy and his partner ended suddenly, although the knowledge of homosexuality being in my family was just beginning.

It was not just my two sisters and cousin that was gay, but now my niece from my oldest sister, whom I've known since she was a baby. I found out about my niece's homosexuality when she was about twenty years old. She started out dating men, got married, but gradually became to like females. She has two children and was raising them with her female partners. My niece is very beautiful and probably never had a problem attracting men OR women. I think that her beauty sometimes leads to her many major setbacks in life. *If all that temptation wasn't there of others trying to get with her, maybe her choices would have been different*, I thought. My niece started showing up at my immediate family gatherings at our houses, and often, she would bring her girlfriend with her. They came to my kid's and grandkids' birthday parties, weddings, graduations, etc. I started to feel as though she and her friend were coming around too much. I felt that I wanted to show love and respect for her; but at the same time, I didn't want her and her friends to be the wrong example for my kids, especially because they would be affectionate toward each other around my kids and grandkids. I tried to explain that point to my wife and kids, and all of them opposed the way I felt. They did not understand why I felt uncomfortable with both of them coming to our house together. I immediately thought that this was proof of how my family had already started to change. *Now they are coming around our home as homosexuals and no one cares?* I thought.

I started to actually feel that they must have some kind of power of persuasion with my family. I had become the bad guy with my family, and my niece and her girlfriend were the victim. *Now something has got to be wrong with this picture*, I thought. The next few times that my niece and her friend came to our house, I tried to restrain my feelings and act as if I wasn't bothered by them. I could see everyone's eyes on me; I suppose they were trying to see what I would say to them. I felt as if my niece and her friend coming to our house as often as they did was done purposely because they knew how I felt about their homosexual relationship. They also probably knew that my family turned against me, and my family was passionate for them. I did not verify my accusations, but I could tell by how they seem unaffected by my attempt to have an attitude toward them. I was hoping that they would be offended by me and not come back, but instead, it seemed that it only made them come around even more. My kids kept asking me, "Dad why are you acting that way"? My wife would respond for me: "He really didn't have to act that way." It seemed that my character was under attack, and I needed to find the right way out of it.

I felt that I was trying to set a good example for my kids by not having homosexuals around my immediate family; but later, it seemed that I was being an even worse example to my kids by the way I was acting toward my niece and her friend. While I was trying to discourage them from coming to my house again, I felt at that time that I did not know what to say or do. It was not like I had not done this before with other people that I did not feel comfortable with. I felt that my kids overlooked my niece and her friend's homosexuality and saw them as being these nice people. They did not care about their sexuality. Now that was sounding familiar to me. *I personally remember being this way before and I was okay*, I thought. I began to talk to my wife and kids about how I really felt about my niece and her friend. I explained my story of my past, without details, of course. I tried to convey to them how I felt that it was my duty as a father to protect what they are exposed to and how I felt that I was allowing my niece to influence my family by being around my house so much. I felt as though I had taken a load off of my shoulder by going to my wife and kids with my worries. I felt as though they understood my fears, and they assured me that there was no need to worry.

It seemed that over time, my niece and her friend eventually stopped coming to our houses. I'm not exactly sure why. My wife blames me, and I never asked my kids what their opinions were, so I don't know. Nevertheless, I feel that I could have been better in the way I handled my niece and her friend, although I could have done a lot worse as well. But overall, I did learn that we are *not* taught to hate others by nature as I was taught to hate homosexuals. This for me was proof through my kids that I obviously had not taught them to hate homosexuals. But I felt differently than they did. I tried not to show hate for my niece and her friend's lifestyle as an example; rather, I always tried to demonstrate patience, long-suffering, and love to my niece and her friend. It seems that is what my wife and kids had learned to do, and they display that today.

I felt because of this experience with my niece and her friend, I truly needed to evaluate myself and figure out how I really felt about homosexuals. I needed to know if what I felt was actually what God would want of me or something different. What led me to question my motives was that I did not feel good about myself after my wife and kids questioned the way I acted toward my niece and her friend. I was struggling to understand how I was wrong. I always allowed my niece to come over to my house, and although I might not have always had a good attitude, I was never disrespectful to them. I just don't understand why I couldn't express my point of view about how I felt about their coming to our houses so often. I wondered, "How can that be considered as being unfair to them?" Eventually, my niece moved to Texas, and I have not had her or her friend at my house since. But the experiences that I have had with her and her friend were reminders for me that I still had unresolved issues toward homosexuals. I need to understand why I felt this way and how I can deal with this more peacefully. It was not that I actually hated homosexuals, but I felt that I was being forced to deal with an issue at my home that I did not feel comfortable with. I did not want to make a decision to tell them to come or go; I just never wanted them to come in the first place. I felt as if they were bringing their personal issues to my house and that it was wrong for them to do that.

My wife and kids made me feel that I was rude to them, and my attempts to defend myself were not effective. I must admit that this was so unexpected. In one way, I was proud that they were not like me in the way I've treated homosexuals; but on the other hand, I feared what might happen if they became to be close to my niece and others like her.

However, the relationship with my other gay sister establishes the fact that it is possible to overcome these barriers that divide us. In fact, other than my wife, she has been my greatest supporter in my writing of religious books. I feel that our ability of being able to overcome our barriers was because we both decided to look beyond what divided us—or maybe ignore what divided us could be a better description for how I actually felt. With the eldest of my gay sisters, it seems that our personalities are similar in some ways, and that is one reason why we are so close. She is gentler in her approach with me compared to my younger sister who is more hostile. If my eldest sister of the two is upset at someone, she is calmer in the way she handles others and herself as compare to the younger sister. I think that my youngest sister's unresolved issues with me are because of the way I viewed her homosexuality in the past. The mutual way that we communicate through my daughter has for now served for us as a temporary solution. Learning how to love gays is just as difficult as it is learning how to love anyone else, it seems. Nevertheless, my two different relationships that I do have with my two gay sisters should serve as evidence of what can happen in our relationships while we are trying to adjust because of homosexuality.

It's clear that we process the ability to be able to reason with each other; it's just the question of whether we choose to do that. It's also obvious that we *choose* to hate others. It is our choice we make, and no one can force us to make that decision. It is possible to love others and not love what they do. I think this is when we become deceived, when we take things so seriously with the things that we don't like in others. We become too critical in enforcing what we do think is approved by God. When we love others, it is a more effective tool to promote change in others, rather than hatred and fault-finding. This was illustrated in my relationship that remains healthy with my one sister who is gay. We both treated each other with respect for our belief and opinions, and we both always showed respect for each other, even if we disagreed with each other on our unresolved issues. It is as if I knew that I needed this relationship to work, and it took that type of attitude to help make my relationship with my eldest gay sister to be successful.

My youngest sister's relationship with me is still under construction. The important thing is that I haven't given up hope of overcoming our differences. My belief is that we should always seek the true essence of what God intended for us to do and that is to love others as we love ourselves, and also we can all claim victory in our lives when we can demonstrate love for those we otherwise would not love.

8

Why Are We So Concerned with How Others Live?

Most of us would agree that our quality of life would be more enriched if we were less concerned over how people live their lives, whether it is over someone that we are in a close relationship with or someone that we don't totally know. Our negative statements about them to us may seem as if it is harmless to others. What we fail to understand is how it affects those that we victimize when we are bothered with how they live their lives. Our kindness that we do share with others every day is like a honey bee whose daily job is pollinating different flowers and plants that depend on it for its survival. Our society works similarly. We are all pollinated from the love and kindness of others. Our smile or facial gestures communicate either negative or positive messages to people about what we think of them.

Our experiences from our encounters with others can have everlasting effects on us; even little things like traffic experiences with those we never met before can turn our morning drive to work into a day of depression and confusion. This can all begin just because of how someone we don't know treated us, or maybe it could be because when we wave to someone, the courtesy of a wave back is not returned, especially when we're certain they saw us wave to them. Even if these types of experiences come from strangers or those we work with or those closest to our family. Either way, this demonstrates how we are affected by the negative opinions that people have, even from those we don't know and have never met.

When strangers are polite to us, most of us feel more of a connection with them. Our awareness of this is usually magnified when someone treats us unkindly or disrespectfully. Usually, when this happens, we may consider it as someone acting rude or disrespectful, but most of us can become permanently affected. We may pretend to brush it off, but it can be an experience that we usually never share much with others. We might have wondered before as to why some people may do this or what the motivating factor for some people's behavior is, especially when they are so unsociable to us. However, there have been many people who begin to doubt themselves and question whether they are worthy or valued because of these types of past experiences. Eventually, we become more accepting of other people's criticism out of our low self-esteem. Somehow we must make it essential that we learn as long as we live in a society with other people, we will be exposed to their criticism of us. The actual reasons why some people behave this way may not be as easy to uncover or understand. Although part of our happiness depends on us overcoming negative people and their opinions of us.

Within most of us, a deep desire exists to examine, analyze, and make judgments of others. For some, this behavior began in childhood, a time when we learn the fundamental differences of others. Our analysis of others began, for most of us, at a very young age. From our childhood experience, our minds are molded and developed. We begin to set our very own standards and expectations in what we think of other people. In fact, we may begin to require others to see things the way that we do in their views of life. This develops as we get older, and some of us develop a feeling of superiority or pride in the way they compare themselves to others. Because of this, it is important for us to better understand what the driving force behind this kind of behavior is, especially when our good intentions to help others end up as our condemnation for those that are not living to our standards.

At some point, the question should become, why are we so concerned with the way other people live their lives? Okay, I admit that most of us have a desire to make our world a better place. We claim that we are concerned with how others live as a way of helping them. Let's face it. Some of us believe that our way of life should serve as everyone's example. We seem to expose others and their weaknesses and shortcomings and use them as a way of promoting our superiority over others. Whether we are religious believers or ordinary, everyday people, we all seem to share this personality trait.

In this chapter, I attempt to challenge my readers to discover what motivates all of us when we become concerned with how others live their lives. After we have questioned ourselves and analyzed our motives, we may find the answers that we otherwise may not have known. The reality is that there are those in the world who may live their entire lives without complaining how others live while there are many people who are the exact opposite. Essentially, as we search to find out what drives our need to seek change in others, we begin to see that this process may be really vital for us in understanding ourselves more clearly. If we closely observe, we shall learn that there are those that anticipate others to behave a certain way or look a certain way for them to be considered as equals. There may be many different complex reasons for this way of thinking, but the fact that some are more outspoken than others demonstrates how some people feel that they have earned the authority to correct people. They live on with their lives thinking that they are the authority for how others should live. Those that do this may have become blinded of the person they are or who they have become. By doing this, our focus on other people's affairs begins to take priority over recognizing our own faults.

I must admit that I don't personally care for the habits that most people may have or the particular way some decorate their home or the fashion of some people. I even find differences in the way many people make everyday decisions in their lives, compared to what I would do. However, at the end of the day, I don't really care what others may do in their lives because it doesn't affect me personally, and I can't justify why I would require someone to change their life for me. The fact that we won't always agree with other people's choices is our reality of being part of society; but the question still remains: why are we so concerned about how others live? We could find many different reasons to justify our beliefs of why people need to change. Often, we may think it's our religious or moral duty to change others, while others may see some people with different lifestyles than themselves as a personal threat to their families or our society.

However, one of the things that we all seem to share in common is our opinions of how we think about what others should do or don't do. There could be many different ways how others live their lives that can affect us directly and sometimes indirectly, or most of the time not affect us personally at all. Yet, somehow it still seems to bother us. As a result of this, we often extremely worry about those we love and care for. We are often led by the desire to change others, our schools, our neighborhoods, or our world. It seems important to us that people of the world should do as we think and not as they actually do. We are not only bothered by the way others live their lives but are also bothered by the traditions, cultures, and beliefs of others that are different from our views. There are opinions some of us have of others that can lead to violence and death, stemming from religion, homosexuality, or even an suggestive comment about someone. Our opinions of how others should live are surprisingly about people we don't really know, just as much as those we do.

As a father, I know that there is a difference in how I feel my children should live compared to how I feel about my other loved ones—such as my sisters, brothers, parents, and extended relatives. It's obvious to most of us that the things that our spouses and children may do will often extremely affect us more than our other relatives. However, this may explain why we are more or less concerned with how others live their lives, depending on the level of how close we are to them. It seems that our greatest criticisms of others are from those closest in relationship with us.

I believe that we can be concerned with how others live often out of fear of the unknown, or the thought of potential threat of danger for those we love. Often we feel that we can see things that they cannot see. We feel that our loved ones are less capable of having the ability to navigate through their personal issues than we are. If it is not this kind of danger that we worry about, then often it is the issue of the way our loved ones conduct their lives. At times, this may become difficult for us to explain to them the way that we believe that we see things more clearly about the way they live their life and explaining it in a way that could be understood by them, as well.

As a parent, we may feel that our relationship with our children is the way we maintain our influence in how they live life, as we hope. We can feel out of control when we can no longer influence our opinions on those we love as we have done before. We may feel that in this particular relationship with our children, that it is more of a personal investment that reflects our personal success or failure. We feel their pain, and we bear a great measure of their suffering by having to witness what we consider to be our children's failure to live life as we expect.

One of the common expressions that we may have learned first was, "Mind your own business" or "Stay out of my business" or maybe "Don't be so nosy. It's none of your business." What we seem to imply when we use these words is that someone is putting too much attention into our affairs. Most people that do this feel the need to educate us. It's almost as if someone is taking a parental role in our lives. In fact, the phrase used most often to describe how others invade our privacy is called "being nosy." It's a phrase that was used as a reflex of how we react to the invasion of our space. For example, the word "nosy" is normally used after someone has asked a questioned that was personal to us. It is the way to describe what someone is actually doing. "Being nosey" describes an attack or an offensive act being carried out against us. It is also another way to describe curiosity. Of course, this word can be used for good or evil intentions; however, curiosity is necessary for us as a way to live. If we were not curious over anything, we would lose our desire to live our life. In fact, the word "curious" sometimes reflects mankind's reasons to explore beyond our understanding of complex matters. Without having curiosity, we would not have the inner drive to become a self-starter. Without this, our lives would have less meaning.

Our curiosity is the engine that drives our desire to be concerned with how others live their life. As I said before, this could be used for good or evil. I think the most innocent way to describe how our curiosity is used is an example of children and their curiosity in which they are generally discovering and exploring the unknown with the lack of any preconceived knowledge. What's amazing is that their reasons for being so concerned with how others live are unique and neutral. Most children's curiosity about how others live are things that usually begin with the word "why." Their curiosity will be a question that needs only an answer. Most children and their questions can be a direct link to our curiosity and our questions. I think what's common is our questions that begin with "why." Basically, when we ask this question, we surrender in our claim to know the answer to something, and we humbly ask for advice.

The question 'why' is not only an acknowledgement of our lack of understanding, but it is a way of explaining our intent to find out or discover something. Although this question could be used in a significant way to ask someone a question such as, "Why did they do that?" However, the innocent way it is used is simply when we don't understand something and we need clarification. The word "why" actually seeks to solve a problem or reveal a solution to a question. If the question is answered, it usually reveals the knowledge that we seek to find an answer to. This is necessary for everyone who use it, although it's amazing what we will do or the extreme measures we will take when we seek the answer. Also, if we will carefully analyze this thought, we realize that our desire to know or understand something that we are not familiar with can be a driving force in our need to know *why* things are the way they are. From this, we begin to form the basis for the answer of our questions and our need to ask why.

When we seek to understand why we are so concerned with how others live and understand it from a child's point of view, we can rely on an innocent way of their intent to understand facts. When children are concerned with how others live, it is nothing that they seek to gain from their concern. Their rapid-fire volley of questions beginning with "why" can seem exhausting to answer; yet it highlights their need to understand the unknown. Most children's questions of concern with how others live begin with an attempt to get familiar with their world. The question may begin with them wanting to ask where their mom or dad is and why the things are the way there are. Most times they are the first to wonder why we are sad or happy. Children's innocent ways of being concerned with how we live is the beginning of much of how we gain understanding with using the question "why." It seems as if the way children use the question "why" can be linked to their need to be secure with understanding facts. Their assembly of information is a process compared to completing a puzzle. With enough facts, they eventually become aware and have a clearer picture. Using children as our example can be a way of understanding the origin for how many of us think and feel as well, while we are in search of gaining a deeper understanding of our motivations.

From this, we are able to realize the time we first began to be concerned for someone and why. We begin to understand that our *why* to our questions all began innocently and are part of our way of learning everything in our world. Most children, as they're developing, will have asked many questions beginning with *why*. From doing this, we will basically form a database of explanations to our "why" questions, which are now used as a factual basis for what we believe in. At some point, our innocent questions of why start developing into a different type of "why." This type of the *why* question comes from someone with a developed mind that already has answers to the question. This question of why is more of a warning. Actually, asking the question "Why did you just do that?" is to imply that whatever was done was something off-limits for that person.

As we evolve from childhood to our adulthood, our why questions continue to develop. We might ask questions about certain things, but our questions as to why things are the way they are seem to be more of a request or demand for something. In fact, this "why" question is more of a complaint. That is, why did this happen to me, or why are you doing this? Unlike a child, we no longer just take for granted an answer for why without opposing why things are the way they are. But now, our question has evolved into a demand for change. Our question is no longer a question, but rather a demand for someone to change their behavior. Actually, this is the moment that we begin to challenge others in how they live and what decisions they make.

At this time, we cross over from seeking answers to our questions of why to demanding change or having expectations. This is when our innocence in the way we view things as a child is changed forever. We transform from our childlike innocence to our adult views. From this, it would seem likely that one of our reasons for why we are so concerned how others live begins at this stage in our life. We no longer accept information from others the same as we have before. But now, it is the kind of why that has expectations of someone. It is a question that anticipates a response by the one asking. However, understanding the different reasons why everyone would be concerned with how others live is as complex as every individual's personality, although we can agree with some more obvious examples such as religion, homosexuality, or mixed-race marriages. These subjects have played a more obvious role in our recent history, but they represent a small part in a much larger picture, and it doesn't give a reason for all of our motivations. For example, we may be against someone for their race or religion, but why exactly we are against them is different than why it concerns us, if they do. In other words, why does it bother us what someone does? I'm sure most could give a reasonable explanation to justify why certain things people do are concerning to us, but it doesn't explain our reason for concern. Essentially, why does it disturb our feelings and emotions?

Using the issue of interracial marriages as an example, the question may be, why would that become an issue with someone? If we analyze this subject, we might find that if it bothers us that two people decide to be in union with each other and it makes us angry, at that exact moment we are experiencing the reaction of the way we can be concerned with how others live. The important part of this reaction is when we understand why it concerns us. It's important to realize that in most cases, it won't change our way of life directly. If we are angry at strangers in interracial marriages that we happen to bump into, it would help to know what motivates our anger. If we would take time to figure it out while we were honest with ourselves, the answer can be used as our way to better understand our reasons for this selfish behavior. Often, I don't believe we actually know why it bothers us. In this case, most may claim that they have never been prejudiced before, and that someone's nationality or race has nothing to do with how they feel. Some of us may actually hold religious views that are against being with someone out of their race, or perhaps our family traditions forbid against it. If so, that doesn't give a complete reason for our anger.

Essentially, if we are bothered by something that will not affect us, then the question becomes, why are we so concerned? Maybe we feel that it's against our morals or that it will change our schools or communities for the worse. Perhaps we may express our concern over the potential for criminal activity. Although these may be legitimate concerns, it continues to lack a justifiable explanation for exactly what bothers us or motivates our anger. It's as if our eyes disagree with what we see without knowing why. We may see a mixed-race couple and their family, and different emotions may overcome us. Some of us may feel that a person is a disgrace to their race of people or that it is against their morals. It's as if we are attempting to devalue people because of what we see. It is as if we feel that if we don't agree with the choices of others, then we condemn them. In fact, if we were to examine what we are doing more closely, we actually are condemning someone for something that doesn't affect us personally. What I'm saying is that there are individuals that don't live, eat, or hang with us, and we feel this way because we expect people to do what we think they should do. Basically, we are being nosy.

Why we should be so concerned with what others do is a question we avoid asking ourselves. However, using race as one example doesn't necessarily adequately describe all areas of how we feel about others and what they do. Basically, we all are different and have our independent views about life. When we establish our life principles, we feel that this is the way that everyone should be as well. We can become irritated with others and their ways. We've guided ourselves by the standards we've set for ourselves. Essentially, we use this as our guide for how we conduct our lives and the way we measure or judge others as well. Actually, our views, habits, and traditions guide our lives. The way we do things is the way we expect others to follow. Basically, when we are being nosy or curious about others and their affairs, it's usually motivated by our desire to know why they do whatever it is that disturbs us. If there is nothing that we can be bothered about with someone, this in itself might upset some of us, leading most of us to be curious of others in search of things that we don't like about them. We could admit that there are things about people that irritate us. It may be the way someone dresses, which helps us form our opinion about someone; or it could be someone's personality, which reminds us of something unpleasant. We can form our opinions of someone sometimes without ever talking with them. The visual image of people has been a deciding factor for what kind of person someone is since mankind's beginnings. It is as if someone's appearance dictates how we categorize their importance.

When we examine more closely our motivation for being concerned with how others live, this may give us the answer that we subconsciously hold. I believe that we operate under different levels of concern for people that can be healthy or not for us. Essentially, at times we cross a line between having compassion with our concern for others or not. I believe it's normal to be concerned for someone we know if they're sick, have domestic issues, need someone's help, or have financial needs. Ultimately, our concern to help others who face this kind of dilemma is a natural and healthy concern to have for someone. At some point down the line, we may feel that this same individual is rude, lazy, filthy, and has no manners. Maybe we didn't know this at first, and now that we do, our interest in this person has evolved. Because of this, our focus is on the negative things about this person that irritates us and our compassion to help has faded and been replaced with our irritation over what bothers us. This is when we feel that it's necessary to give our opinion over what irritates us. There can be many different things people do that irritate us without our being conscious of how we feel. We can be bothered by the young kid who we saw walking down the sidewalk with a hoodie and his pants hanging under his backside, or maybe we don't like the person we see that has a body full of tattoos. We may feel that these individuals violate the basic dress code, or that they are individuals that are untamed or radical.

Our image that we have of those different from us can influence the way we think. We probably never took a moment to question ourselves and ask, why do I care what others do? Actually, we may deny that we do care, but our concern with how others live might be obvious to others around us. If we could recognize that we are affected by our opinion of others and if we are honest and willing to admit how we actually think in certain situations on this subject, we can gain a different perspective of understanding. Essentially, I feel it's important for us to understand why we are concerned with how others live and why it bothers us. If we are truthful with ourselves, we would admit that our eyes expose all the things that appeal to us as well as the things that don't. But what we do or how we react to what doesn't appeal to us is what's worth understanding. The kid walking down the street with the hoodie and his pants hanging half down may draw different reactions from different people. Most senior adults will be more critical in their views than the younger adults; both groups will have quite different views.

It seems that the younger generation will react differently and is more liberal in their views in supporting this much differently than senior adults. Nevertheless, understanding their level of concern and why they are so different may reveal our motivations. From this, maybe we can receive a clearer explanation for why we are so concerned with how others live. Our younger generation is one that is more acceptable of the diversity than any other generation before. The question is *why*. I'm sure it's obvious that they were not raised as strictly as our seniors were, and I'm also sure that the value system of our society was quite different seventy years ago than it is today. This may give credence to the idea that we learn these values from our environment, and that this is not a personal choice but something that our outside environment created.

It's a fact that the older adult has more memory of the past and more experience, but there is also the suspicion that there is a generational divide between both views. It's obvious that those with the least amount of age and experience are more likely to be more accepting of the way people dress or of their tattoos. It is as if change is clear and uninterrupted in our view. We might consider that if these were our children, we would have more of a right to voice our opinion. We may feel more connected with what irritates us most. Despite what we feel, most likely if we do this, children will claim that we are getting in their business or that we are overreacting. They themselves will one day ask their parents the question, why are we so concerned with how they live? Despite our claim of being justified because we raised them or that we love them, our efforts can be considered as invasive with our good intentions. We can often feel helpless in our efforts to change someone that we care for.

The things in life that we feel are normal may not be what our kids feel comfortable with and vice versa. Despite this, most of us will be reluctant to consider other options that are different from theirs. It is as if we are taken over by our need to be correct. When we are concerned with how others live, we attempt to influence our method and solution for their challenges. We become their advisor, counselor, and consultant. Our offered services to others can become the way we validate who we are to ourselves and others. It may be easier to understand why we might have concern over how others live, especially those who are related to us more closely, such as family. However, it is worth pausing to understanding the reason why. I mean, I'm just trying to understand how some can justify things they believe that are so outrageous and seemingly out of touch with reality.

Understanding more clearly why we are so concerned with how others live requires our personal effort to accomplish. It will require us to be truthful and also will allow our thoughts to be clearer. Because of this, what we do will be more visible to us. There are several examples beginning with religion, family, marriage, and friends that can be a more practical reason for our concern over others and how they live; however, knowing what activates our thoughts is what is vital to understand. If it's religion that has influenced our way of thinking about others, most may expect something like this to be a more common thing. We already may think that our guideline is our traditions from our religious beliefs, as most are strongly influenced in a particular way to live from their religion and by the laws of their beliefs, and although when we use it for how we live our lives, it then becomes the instrument for how we gauge others.

Religion can be used as a method of condemning others for how they live their lives, and we are able to blame religion without having to take responsibility in our condemnation of people and their values. Essentially, we hide behind the laws of religion as our reasons for what we do. Religion has supported mankind's justification for the way we have persecuted others in the past, and it will continue in the future as a result of our association in religion. We have become insensitive to others and their beliefs and opinions. We have become desensitized for people's feelings and how they wish to live. For example, in the past it was not acceptable for females to wear pants in my church. Although today, there are those who may find that to be insulting. However, it does highlight a point of how everyone in our church was intensely against it then, but allows it now. Some religious leaders were so against it at that time and also used biblical scriptures to support their views, but today they now support women who dress this way, which, for me, is confusing to completely understand why.

If although, we use this as another example of how we were concerned with how others live, we can better understand why. Women traditionally did not dress with pants. The impression to most was that it was a form of masculinity, and a dress was a form of a female being feminine. People of religion were passionately concerned about women who unknowingly would violate this unwritten dress code. I guess the concern was not just that a woman was dressed as a man, but more so that it was presenting ourselves before God in an informal manner when we should otherwise honor Him formally with our best. Our concern for how others dressed seemed to be more of an expectation that represented no biblical value, and as a result, it has evolved as our concern for how others live, as well.

When we are concerned with how others live that are family connected, can be perhaps the most difficult thing for us to deal with and because of that fact alone, we may feel that we have some investment to protect or that we have the designated authority to correct our loved ones. With family, we can often be more judgmental than with others. It's not as if we intend this, but more so that we are emotionally involved when we voice our opinions. We can deceive ourselves with having the intentions to help others often avoiding judging or condemning them of their failures or mistakes. With family, our link from our childhood is often what intensifies our need to be concerned for how our loved ones live. It's something that has a past and present connection for us. Even with family, not all are always as close and the family disputes themselves are proof of our expectations of others. Essentially, family arguments are a result of our concern over what others do or don't do that bothers us. Sometimes this is the example of our attempt to enforce our opinions upon others. I'm sure most disagreements with family begin this way—that is, with anger over what someone expected from someone else. Ultimately, our anger for others is essentially for things they did or did not do that we expected of them. I mean, if we were not concerned at all with what others do, then in reality we would not have any concern with them and their affairs. But we must admit that our concern for our immediate family and how they live is of more concern to us than our distant relatives. It's safe to say that our concern for our spouses or our children are more sacred to most of us, and our expectation for this part of our family is unique. Most will agree that we are totally more passionate over how others live in this situation.

Our friends are a perfect example of how we are so concerned with how others live. In fact, our friendships are an example of what we expect. It is based on our expectation that the relationship is more personal with them than with anyone else. Also, a friendship is a commitment to be faithful to someone else. In fact, it is the primary reason why anyone would consider someone else as a friend, and most of the time, it's expected that you will be closer to them than most others. Factually, it gives more clarity on why maintaining a friendship is more difficult than most may imagine. Our relationship with friends operate on the mutual agreement that both will be concerned with each other on what we do in our friendships. The relationship is special because it fulfills our expectations of what we consider a friend to be. When it stops and no longer fulfills our expectations, is when it's more noticeable that we are all in some way concerned with how others live for different reasons in and out of friendships. We begin to blame others for the failure of our friendships. It could be because of something as simple as someone forgetting your birthday that could trigger a stormy relationship with a friend or the failure of a friend to acknowledge you when you are in a relationship. From this, it's clear that we have expectations for others in our friendships.

Essentially, we are concerned with how our friends live based upon our expectations of them. In fact, the relationship's ability to thrive is solely based upon both to fulfill each other's expectations. When we do this, we are actually being unique in how we treat our friends compared to everyone else. It is a result of this mutual affection that makes a friendship what it is. But understanding why we are concerned with strangers and those that we have never met are worth our consideration It could be the youth with his loud music coming from his vehicle or the bum asking for money on the corner that irritates us. At some point, we should ask ourselves why we are so concerned with what strangers do. It seems that they would be the last on our list of people that affect us. I mean, they should be because we don't know them; they are strangers. Yet we are affected and angered by the car in front of us driving slowly in traffic, the person in line in a grocery store giving the clerk a hard time, or the person talking too loud in a movie theater. These are the types of strangers that can affect most of us without even considering that they are strangers. We act on impulse as if we should protect or correct others when they oppose our views.

For anyone to have an opinion about or feel angry at someone who is a stranger is worth analyzing. The reason for our expectations for strangers to follow our views, whether it is making sure that someone drives the speed limit or that someone cuts their weeds in their yard. We find ourselves angry at people we have never met. Our opinions of strangers are just that—opinions. It does not necessarily and actually represent who they are. It only represents our idea of what we don't like in what we see in the people we meet. Actually, when we are concerned with how strangers live, what we really expect is for others to live the way we would. We seek to make sure everyone disciplines their children or obeys the traffic laws as we do, or maybe we are irritated at those that are responsible for the wandering dog in the neighborhood or the neighbor with junk cars in the front yard.

Most of our frustrations over people in our daily lives come from those that we never met. The strangers of this world will essentially always exist in our lives—appearing, disappearing, and leaving their footprints as part of our journey and experiences. The most popular strangers that we know and never met are the famous people that we see or hear on television or radio, although we feel a connection with them because of their music or movies.

The fact is that they are strangers to us. Despite this, we are drawn to them because of their talent or that they are famous. These strangers can potentially influence and shape our views and beliefs. It seems that we unknowingly can be overwhelmingly passionate with these types of strangers. Our concerns for the way these individuals live their lives have deep meaning for some people. Often, we look up to these strangers, and what we expect of them is that they do not fail us. We expect these strangers to be the person we saw on television or the voice we saw and heard singing a popular song. Ultimately, we are impressed with these types of strangers, and often, we are concerned with how they live because it is the foundation for the way we measure our worthiness. They have become a guideline for us to measure who and what we wish to be. Another big reason why some are so concerned with how these strangers live is because without them there is no example to follow. Our dependence on someone to show to us the latest fashion trend or the most up-to-date events or trends is our source from which everything popular originates from. We are changed by these influences, and most of the time we are molded and shaped by strangers who influence us with their fame, fashion, and talent.

Although, understanding why we are so concerned with how others live is more complex than one might expect. With most people, it begins out of their desire to help others. For some, their religious belief usually is the backbone that supports this desire to help others. In the early stages, most religious people's concern for others begin with a genuine and honest intent to help others, but it later develops into a more aggressive approach to enforce their belief. Their desire to help other people develop into their condemnation for what they see in others that irritates them. I suppose most religious people's concern for how others live their lives are borne out of what their religion requires of them. Their belief has influenced their reasoning after being programmed to its traditions of its religion. Because of this, we fail to be independent in our views or thinking of what we do believe. As religious followers we are trapped in between trying to follow what we are taught to be the right way to live and understanding those who don't agree with our belief. Our moral beliefs have led us to believe that anyone living different from our belief is immoral. We have become a person that opposes others and their way of life as a direct result of what we have learned.

Often, as religious followers, we are against the people that we should support. Normally, this is a result of our concern over how others think and believe that conflicts with us and what we were taught from our religious belief. Our attempt to help others because of this often ends up being perceived as our demand for their change. Religious people who are concerned with how others live their lives and their attempt to help is often interpreted by others as their method of invading our privacy. This becomes delicate and extremely difficult when our religious views are being articulated as advice for someone. Ultimately, most people are receptive to what we have to say until our subject is about their affairs. When it becomes personal, it feels as if someone is being invasive. What is difficult is understanding why someone is so concerned with the homosexuality of others. If I were asked why I was so concerned about my sisters being homosexuals, it would be difficult to explain. For me to answer this would require two different answers for both of my sisters.

The youngest one is the one that I will use as my first example. One of the reasons why I was so concerned with her homosexuality in the beginning years of her life change are much different than present. It began out of my concern of what I thought was not a healthy homosexual relationship mainly because of the recent divorce with her husband. I also thought it was unusual for her to switch genders. It took time for me to actually understand that this was normal behavior for others. Also, I felt concerned for her out of my brotherly love, and her ex-husband who was now also my ex brother-in-law that she replaced with her female partner. I know that it was her private affair that I'm giving my opinion about, yet it affected me and what seemed so normal with her relationship with her husband. I was bothered about her new relationship. I actually felt jealous in the beginning. My intentions were not to be invasive; rather, it was an attempt to understand what and why she was doing these types of things with her new relationship. In the beginning it caught me off guard. I mean, it's not like there were clues or warning signs about my sister's potential homosexuality that I knew of. Although, getting adjusted to this change required time for me to reflect on everything that had affected her.

I thought that one of the most persuasive reasons for my concern for the way my sister lives her life is how I felt within me. I also thought that the feeling that I had within me is something that caused an involuntary negative response. At that time, it appeared as if I was not in control over how I felt emotionally. I suppose that can be a leading factor for some of our problem, and that is trying to understand why we feel certain ways and trying to control how we feel. When we finally do figure out certain elements of how we feel or why, trying to control or change how we feel still remains our biggest challenge. It seems from this that we could begin to realize just how we are being influenced and led by our feelings. Despite this, understanding my reasons for being concerned about my sister being gay required me to concentrate on my motivation for wanting her to change. My first task of trying to articulate why I felt so concerned itself became difficult, as it was trying to defend my reasons for having any concern at all. It was as difficult as it is explaining to someone why you feel awkward about something. Just the word *awkward* itself implies that you feel off-balance or unprepared for the moment. Yet, that is how I felt. However, what I am able to articulate more clearly is what I thought when I reacted to the knowledge of my sisters' homosexuality and how I evolved years later. It started out as an emotional shock when I discovered she was gay, and that in itself led to an adjustment of my reality of her, which also required the rehabilitation of our relationship. I first realized the things that were once of interest to her have evolved, but finding just how it has changed is the challenge that is necessary for me and others, which has proven to be more difficult to acquire than what we may first imagine.

Trying to fight the thought that she was different and somewhat of a stranger to me is what I felt at first. I never figured out why I felt sad or depressed, but eventually I overcame it. It was clear that out of my confusion about her homosexuality that it was an issue with me, and I suspected that it may have been the reason why I felt guilty of pretending to accept something that I was fundamentally disturbed about. I did not want to admit my jealousy of her gay friends; my excuse for this was hid in my false smiles and empty hugs that I extended to them. When they were present, I reserved complaining about my dislikes, as I waited for the best opportunity to be effective in revealing how I felt about them. The problem was that I thought that I had insufficient facts to support my opposition about her homosexuality. It was frustrating enough that I could not articulate my feelings, but it was worse that I lacked the arsenal of facts to go to war with her over my dislikes about her life.

Explaining and understanding why I'm so concerned over my sister's homosexuality was something that actually took years for me to begin to feel as if I understood, and almost as long to understand why I felt that way about my sisters. I guess my goal of overcoming the feeling of embarrassment around certain people—is something we will all face and eventually overcome as well. Our pride has got to be broken. Unfortunately, this is a time when we don't have answers for solving something like this that affects us. We eventually learn to surrender, at least in talking negatively to our victims about this subject, even though we have not changed in how we condemn it within our thoughts. Despite this, I continued to be concerned over how my sister lived. But I continued to evolve in the way I felt as time passed. My sister's boldness became more in-your-face. She made clear her opposition to those that did not agree with her homosexuality. We both stopped communicating with each other for years. For me, my lack of communication with her was an attempt to avoid conflict over our unsettled differences. My feelings were that she should respect how I felt as I should respect hers. At that time, I began to feel as though my feelings did not matter to her, only my acceptance of her change and knowing that they have my respect for their homosexuality.

The problem was that my youngest sister's rebellious personality is a trait that I share as well, and it became a wedge that continues to divide us. I felt as if my sister was intentionally aggressive in demanding my acceptance of her choice, and because of that I grew defensive over time. When I would attempt to let go of my concern for the way she lives, I often confused this with letting go of my love that I have for her. I felt that I was basically attempting to desensitize myself from what she does while doing this. Perhaps, it basically is the same as shutting down and having feelings for her with the intent of not being concerned with how she lives. *Maybe that is what a lot of other people may do*, I thought. We totally shut down in our relationships instead of dealing with the reality of the change with those we love. There are some people who just refuse to emotionally deal with the subject. I think that these are the individuals who will shut down to hide their feelings, or maybe protecting it may be what some do. I can really relate to this. In fact, it really takes a bolder person who by nature has the ability to loudly voice their opinions to others without fear. Personally, this was difficult for me—that is, "speaking my mind," as they say. I could never find the voice to tell my sisters anything, especially if I felt it might hurt them. I guess you could say that I was pretending to be something that I wasn't. I felt intimidated by her boldness about her homosexuality. It was clear to me you can expect a battle if you oppose her views.

It was hard to ignore the fact that before her homosexuality was an issue to me, that we were close. I did not understand how and at what point the change occurred. Although it seemed to me as if I was reacting to the change with her that I was not creating it. I felt my proof was the fact that before I realized her homosexuality, we never had problems between us and I felt this change was somewhat responsible. Understanding why I was so concerned with how she was living her life was more difficult than articulating why I felt this way. I felt explaining my thoughts and being dramatic about it was easier than facing the facts. At some point, it was hard to ignore that I felt a loss; and because of this disconnection, I blamed others that were closer to her than I was. Ultimately seeing her homosexual relationship with others blossom caused a sense of rejection within me. It was as if she found support for who she was despite how I felt. Although that is the way it should be. Despite this, I felt deprived of her because of what divided us.

At some point, I had to be honest with myself and ask myself the question of whether my problem was that I wanted my sister to be what I expected and if so, was I being selfish about something personal to her? I had to face the fact that society had changed and that I was the minority in my opinion of her homosexuality. Part of what irritated me about this was that her choice and the controversy that surrounds it has caused our division. I couldn't stop thinking about the way she was before this, and it was difficult to understand how she could change. It appeared easier for others to accept this change with her than I was, but I was struggling to think it through. I couldn't understand how you could have two desires for male and female partners. This was new to me, and it was difficult to comprehend how it was possible. Up until that time, I could never have imagined anything that could have been a challenge to our relationship. Before this, I never experienced any disagreement of any kind with her, so knowing how to navigate through all of this became difficult. Nevertheless, I felt that her choice to be gay caused a conflict with our belief and traditions, and therefore it led to our disagreement with each other. Absent of this, there was nothing else to blame for what was dividing us.

Despite all my reasons for being against her homosexuality choices, I still had difficulty coming up with compelling enough reasons to use as a tool in a debate with her over this issue. So my complaints about her were limited to how she made me feel. I had to admit that she affected my emotional state of being, but she was of no other threat to me. What disturbed me more was that I felt that there was something else about what she was doing that bothered me that I just could not point out. As I search for the words to express how I felt, it always reflects back as it being my opinion or my way of judging her. Understanding why I was so concerned with how she lives her life remains as confusing as understanding her life. Both are unique and challenging.

With my older sister, who is also homosexual, my experience was quite different from the beginning until the present. Discovering that she was gay was just as challenging as my youngest sister, but the total journey was different. But explaining why I am concerned with how she lives her life is just as challenging. They are both the youngest in our family. With the elder sister, it was the first time I had personally dealt with homosexuality in our family. Because of this, there were a lot of elements about my encounter with her that I had not become adjusted to, as I had with my other sister. I was less concerned about the way she lived compared to my youngest sister. One of the reasons why it was difficult for me to be upset about the eldest (of the two) sister's homosexuality was a result of her gentle spirit, and her kindness and how her tone of voice vibrated a calmness that assured me of her love for me. With her, it wasn't hard for me to notice that my concern for how she lived her life would not be easy to explain to her or anyone else. Part of this was because of the perfect way she managed her affairs and her family that in itself made me feel as if I had no authority to advise someone who manages their life better than me. If I set aside using religion as my argument against her homosexuality or her morals and absence of this, it became difficult to explain my reasons for what I feel. I'm limited to describing the way I feel others should live without any source of legitimacy to support my claim. Despite this, it became more difficult understanding my opposition, and it was also difficult adjusting to my emotions.

At that time, society had not accepted homosexuality as it does today, and because of that fact it was easier *not* to support homosexuality equality than it was to be *for* it. In fact, most had a fear of others knowing that they had family members that were gay. I suppose my expectations of thinking that she would be with a man one day were not her fault. It was an expectation that was not formed from a thought-out process. Instead, it was molded from my childhood experiences. I felt as if the script that my sister should play in my part that I had expected for her life was interrupted by the reality of who she actually became. The fact that her decision was final, disassembled my hopes for a different change to occur one day with her. I felt that the results of my prayers were not as effective as I had hoped. This was a sobering moment for me. Actually, I felt a type of hurtful confusion that I could not articulate. I still loved her, but what she was doing in her relationship continuously made me feel conflicted within.

At this moment, I allowed my love to influence and direct my method of the way I responded to her. It felt as if I was a student learning what I should do so I would have less of a chance for a mistake with what I may say. It was obvious to me that putting my negative feelings about her homosexuality to the side would be necessary for me to focus on this challenge. If not, it would dominate my thinking. I thought that this is one of the examples how we could avoid being so concerned with the way others live their lives. Essentially, I was trying to avoid things that could stop or hinder my relationship, as a result of my preconceived thoughts. I tried allowing myself to imagine only positive thoughts about her. The way I treated her would affect the way she thought about me. At that time, the temptation to speak out my opposition about her life at times felt overwhelming for me to contain. But when given the opportunity, I would choke up and lose the courage to reveal what was bothering me.

As I reflect back on this, it seems funny how I never asked questions about her relationships or the reason for her homosexuality. It is as if I conducted my everyday life of being around her while avoiding what bothered or disturbed me. In the beginning, this complex process of understanding why I was so concerned about the way she lived her life was not a thought-out intentional process, rather it was a reflection of my curiosity about her life. I did not feel as comfortable asking her questions about her life directly. I tried to approach this in a different way which was less conspicuous, which required researching and observing everything with my visual observation. I felt that this gave me the ability to understand most things about her more effectively by this process. It also allowed me to focus on what I have experienced instead of what I presumed about her. With this way of doing things, I became more of an observer and not the conductor of her life. My observation became a learning tool that I used to become more aware of something that I did not fully understand or agree with. This process has allowed me to relate to something that otherwise I would not relate to. I was forced to admit that I was powerless to control the things that interest my sister regarding her relationships. However, I felt that if I observed what her friends did that intrigued my sister, that could be a way of understanding them.

I always knew that we would one day grow older and live our lives with our immediate families; however, my early expectation was that later in life she would have a husband and kids. It's not that I didn't like her life's partner; it's only what I had anticipated before I knew of this. I believe a big concern I had about her homosexuality is out of that expectation. I felt that it's already hard relating to my sister because she is a female, but with her having a husband to me would be sort of a male extension of her and could have helped me to more effectively relate to her, and I think that it is hard to repeat that with her gay partner. Having a male partner would most likely have created a mutual connection between he and I that would allow us to go places and do things together, obviously doing what men usually do, as it might not be possible with her female partner. Ultimately, I could not find the words to explain that a female partner cannot replace a male partner because of the unique way men relate. Although, the thought of explaining this to them seemed a bit of an out-of-line thing for me to talk about, instead silence was the way in which I dealt with it. Nonetheless, it's not as if there was a friendship problem with her female partner; I couldn't expect anything different from her or her partner. It's just what it was at that time, and it's something I no longer question. I ultimately want my sister to be happy and fulfilled in her life. So far, her life partner seems to definitely complete her expectations, so how can I expect anything else of her? *To do so would make it seem as though she was living purposely to please me or others*, I thought. However, understanding why I was so concerned with the way my sister lives her life was the issue that I needed to better comprehend. Even though I had expectations of what I thought she should do in her relationship, it was becoming clear that it was information that my sister could continue to politely avoid. My notion of her having a male partner to me seemed to be a better match for her, although it also demonstrates my lack of concern for what she wanted when I thought like this. In particular, it reflects how this can be so confusing for us to digest, but it gives the reason why most of us will fight for the change of someone so passionately without considering how they felt or exactly what the reality of the possibility of the change we seek from them is absent of what they desire.

My eldest sister of the family is straight and is married to her husband of thirty-plus years. My sister has a daughter and granddaughter, which starts another issue. The issue of my niece and my niece's daughter, who are both homosexuals as well, was something that was a major change for my eldest sister. Despite this, she continued to teach values in her home to her daughters and granddaughter(s), and I could not understand how her daughter and granddaughter became homosexuals or bisexual. It seemed important to me for others to question. The reason why a mom, grandma, or uncle would be so concerned with how loved ones should live, I think should be worth understanding. Although, as an uncle, my feelings are different than that of my eldest sister's and how she feels because obviously those are her children, even despite the fact that I love them also as their uncle. However, having this type of relationship with them reminded me of how I dealt with my two sisters' and their homosexuality. I immediately began to question why was this was happening to our family. I was just beginning to come to terms with my two sisters, and now I'm dealing with a newer generation. Yet, now it was my sister's kids and grandkids, although I was limited in my involvement with their everyday lives. Despite this, I was around enough throughout the years to watch them grow from childhood through adulthood.

Within these years, I was able to observe the way my sister and her husband evolved when dealing with the homosexuality of their kids and grandkids directly in their home. I felt as if I always tried to extend my help as an uncle to advise them, but my sister would never be open to that kind of closeness with her family. She kept guarded what ultimately would become known to everyone, and that was that her daughter and granddaughter were gay. When we came to her house or she to my house for events, my sister kept her kids occupied enough so I could not talk with them about the details of their lives. Through the years, some of the changes in her daughter and granddaughter became noticeable to me when they were around the ages of eleven or twelve with their social interests, behavior, friends, outfits, and hairstyles. Although I suspected that these could be signs of their homosexuality, I thought it would be wise not to elaborate on my actual thoughts to her or to my sister. Although, it was different with my sister's great attempt to keep this concealed from me and others, attempting this was an indication to me that she was very emotional over what was happening with her family. I think one of my reasons for having concern was the way it affected my sister's well-being as well as several smaller reasons I may have had.

Over the years, I believe my sister's attempt to discipline and debate with her children over their homosexuality has only led to division within their relationships. I don't think she has been able to find peace within herself because of their lifestyles that goes against our Christian values. In the beginning, she went through the faze of blaming herself and questioning her maternal skills as the factor for this, or maybe as the reason for her disappointment with them. My niece's life that she shared with other women we felt was another issue that my sister was troubled by. My niece's attempt to raise her own daughter without this kind of influence is something my sister was hoping would not repeat itself with them. For me, this felt as if it was another devastating moment for her family at least as far as I was concerned at that time. My niece and her daughter were a joy to be around. Although, my niece's energy level seemed to be at its highest peak when she was around. Her love for makeup, beauty, and fashion was reflected in the way she dressed, although she and my sister seemed to frequently be at odds over different issues of their lives. However, their love for each other could still be noticed. If asked, my sister would confess that the homosexuality of my niece and her daughter has always been a major cause of concern for her, and also has been a road-blocking ability to express herself effectively about their homosexuality. She has lost the battles and the war with them, and throughout that process her best defense was using her belief in religion, but her talk about her religious beliefs over time have become an old broken record that reflects the same message over and over to them. Although her family has always been part of the church, it appeared as if my niece had found different religious views. Because of this, my niece did not respond well to those who bought the controversial subject of religion up as the topic for conversation with her.

I think for many years my sister tried to overcome how she felt about her daughter's homosexuality by ignoring the reality of it. As my niece grew older it became too much for my sister to deal with, so she became withdrawn and didn't discuss it much with anyone. It appeared to have gone in flow with all the other problems of her life that she had to deal with, although to me, it seemed as if everything was seemingly happening all at once. I believe my sister used every technique that she could imagine on her daughter and granddaughter that she felt would change them from their homosexuality. I'm certain she discussed every topic on homosexuality that there was to talk about with them, as well. Although, understanding the reasons she was so concerned with why her daughter and granddaughter are gay can be best understood by looking at it from a maternal perspective. My sister's reason for concern for her child and grandchild was out of her love, as with any other parent. The vision she imagined for her child's future was altered by her homosexuality, even though her daughter may have expressed how she was more fulfilled by this way of life.

Despite this, my sister with the aide of her disappointment made it impossible for her to accept this new way of life. In fact, after having a lengthy talk with my sister about this subject, I learned that she felt intimidated by her daughter and others because of her opposition to homosexuality. She says that it felt as if society was forcing homosexual equality on us. She felt this way because of the lack of support that everyone has given her in dealing with the homosexuality of her family. Ultimately, my sister feels that she cannot verbalize to most people about her opposition of being against homosexuality without being attacked for her belief. She also feels that she has to be careful of anything she says around her daughter and granddaughter that may be offensive to homosexuals. Finally, she feels as if her religious freedom is taken away when she is in her home or when she is around them. It's not as if my sister cannot express her religious beliefs around them, but rather that her daughter rejects my sister using religion as a way of belief for her life. My niece and her mom's relationship have not fully recovered because of this issue. Although despite my sister's opposition to their homosexuality, she was committed to the completion of raising her granddaughter until she graduated. The fact that my niece was gay did not stop my sister from her commitment for her granddaughter or in giving her a home in her house. It was clear that my sister had unconditional love for her family, regardless of her opposition in their life. She showed persistent effort to continue to be part of their lives, and she has not given up on caring for them despite how she felt. In the beginning, when my niece's daughter was a young teenager, my sister felt at the time that society may have seen her granddaughter capable of making her own choices of who to love at that age, my sister saw it as something that was a threat to her future and that her granddaughter's choice to focus on her desires to be with other girls was something that was not appropriate.

My sister admits that her granddaughter does very well with her grades in school and that she excels in sports. She often seeks attention from my sister with her school sports. My sister explains to me how difficult it is when her granddaughter expects attention or for her to be proud of what she is involved in. She understands that my great-niece is trying to seek this attention, but my sister says it's difficult to tell her that she is proud of her life and the way she lives because of how disappointed and hurt she was over her homosexuality. It's sort of conflicting. In one way, she is proud that her granddaughter is doing well in school and in sports, but my sister's ultimate goal for my great-niece is for her to act as a female as she was born to be, which was actually more important to my sister than seeing her success in school. It was as if her granddaughter's reasons for doing so well in school was just to please my sister. Seeing this happen to my sister's family was heartbreaking at times. It was as if all of them wanted and needed confirmation that they were a good mom, daughter, or granddaughter. They needed each other's love and support, but instead, they seemed to blame each other for the disappointments of their life.

Trying to understand the reason for my sister's concern for how her daughter and granddaughter lived seemed something that was surprisingly important to do. It actually highlights a perspective about homosexuality for me, that most never considered, and especially the various ways in how others are affected by those they love that are homosexuals. We begin to realize that they also have a story, and when they pursue it most are faced with controversy and are demonized for their personal opinions regarding their loved ones. It's not as if my sister or others like her made a selective choice to be against homosexuality; but by random choice they had to deal with this challenge, whether they agree with it or not. My sister explained to me her regret about the way she condemned her children in the past over their homosexuality, but getting her to understand that she was just doing what she thought was best at that time is what was most important to me. It was clear from all of this that my sister wasn't ever able to come to peace with the homosexuality of her family. It seemed that her struggle was to understand how it all went from bad to worse with her attempt to create change in her family. Her disappointments were an indication that she has not found the way to accept her children in that capacity, and she continues to search for understanding and the way to cope with it. My sister's experience with her family is an example of her reasons why she justifies her concern with how her family lives their life. Although with each of us, our experiences come with its unique story. This was a story of a mother who has concern for her daughter and granddaughter who are gay.

However, the story of how my aunt was concerned with her sons that were also homosexuals is a story worth our time to read. My aunt was a mother of eight children, and six of them were male. Two of her sons were openly gay, and the rest were straight. None of the remaining boys were ever married or had known kids. The reasons I use her as an example of why someone would be so concerned with how others live is because of her expectations as a mother who has multiple sons. A mother's expectations and love for her boys are unique and even more so when they are homosexuals. It demonstrates the extent that a mom will go to support her sons. With my aunt, it was not different. Knowing that my cousin was gay was something I later discovered when I was an older adult because I lived in California, and he was raised in Colorado. We met several times when we younger, but I was not raised around him or his brothers. When my siblings and I met our cousins, the subject was about playful things such as playing different sports at the park or in the streets of my aunt's house. Our exposure to their lives was always cut short because we were only visiting and lived in another city. But the memories of my aunt are precious because of the warmth and love she extended to us. Her cooking and advice allowed me to experience a motherly aspect of her personality. She treated me as if I was one of her own. This closeness to her led me to better understand how she reacted to certain elements of my cousins' homosexuality. My aunt, as others in my family, are part of a religious belief that traditionally has been against many things including homosexuality. Despite this, she continued to unconditionally love her sons who were gay. I'm sure she had her challenges about it, but over the years, I could never figure that out.

As her nephew, she knew that I had married my wife at nineteen years of age and had children already. I was already married to my wife of thirty-six years (at that time it was fifteen years), and we had four children between us, and we now have more than twelve grandchildren as well. Her six sons are now already over fifty years old with no children, which means no grandchildren. I say this to explain how being around my aunt and realizing that she is much older than me and that she has no known grandchildren by her sons made me think that perhaps my presence reminded her of what she does not have from her sons and only having one grandchild from her daughter. Nonetheless, it became easier to understand why a mom like my aunt would be concerned with how her children lived their lives. I feel that her concern for the way her boys lived their lives was with the intent to help, so she could one day see them raise their own children. The expectations of my aunt of hoping that her sons would one day have a relationship with a female and do the things that a husband and father would do seemed like a normal thought. As a result of that, I begin to ask myself, Is it unfair to her sons with the way my aunt thought? Even though her intentions were for her children to one day leave home and live how she thought, which was for them to be different than they are now. Despite this, I think that her expectation that all of them would be straight instead of gay is what the factor was for how she thought.

I felt that most mothers instinctively expect that their sons will have a family, be a father, and raise kids. I thought that maybe this process would remind them of moments shared with their dad and because of this is something that they hope would happen as well for their sons and grandsons to experience also. As a cousin to my aunt's kids, I was closer to the boys that were straight. It was not a conscious choice, but they were usually more obvious to us as someone fun to be with when we came in town to visit. But there was a difference in the way our relationship with them was compared to my cousins who were gay. After discovering that these cousins were homosexual, I remember that they showed a sense of insecurity in the way they responded when I was around them. My cousins who were straight were much louder and assertive than their brothers who were gay. I thought they were quiet and seemed at times as if they were withdrawn from our conversation. Of course, their interests were not the type of stuff that most boys would discuss, such as cars, girls, or sports. It seemed that the ones that were homosexual never expressed what their interests were to me personally. One was soft-spoken, and as I said before, he was not the type that would discuss that hidden part of themselves to others. But one of my other cousin, who is also gay, was completely different from his brother. He was outspoken and fun to be around. It seemed as if he went to the extreme when it came to drama and excitement in his life. He lived life to the fullest. Nevertheless, they mutually seemed satisfied with their lives and happy throughout their homosexual relationship.

They both ultimately had difficulty in connecting with their relatives outside of their immediate family. Most of my other cousins who were straight felt that their lives were controversial and that their homosexuality was condemned by their family and belief in religion. Most of our outside family never spoke much about it. They unconsciously did not allow their kids and family to mingle with my cousins who had siblings that were gay. Of course, it was done this way so that no one would be able to pinpoint the reason why they purposely avoided mingling too close to their family, and certainly, no one in my family would ever admit that they had done this. Although despite what they may claim, I am describing what I saw as I remember it. I don't think this was done because everyone thought their relatives were bad people. It was because most of my uncles and aunts raised their families with deep religious traditions and beliefs that taught against homosexuality. In fact, some of my uncles and aunts were insecure about letting my cousins come around our large family, which was before anyone knew about my sisters' homosexuality. The point I'm trying to make is that although most of my relatives may have judged my cousins for *their* homosexuality, the same ones also treated *our* family the similar way. I sometimes think that some religious people just go too far in their practices and beliefs from their religion, and they fail to understand the priority of it, which is to first love and treat others the same as we expect for ourselves instead of avoiding those who are different as if in fear of being infected by them. As a family, we fail to show loved ones that their lives were significant to us despite their homosexuality. Also, our silence is just as bad, not saying anything to someone sends them a similar message as not being of importance to us, or that they are not equally part of the family. Most of this practice was done by the older generation of our family whose values were strict and judgmental.

The fact that my family's values and beliefs are against homosexuality, they would say is supported by our religion. However, I believe it is the reason why we need to understand that the controversy about it must make it difficult for everyone to navigate through, especially when we comprehend that our belief and the religious beliefs of many are in direct conflict with the belief in scriptures of the Bible. Understanding this point allows us to better relate to the commitment that is necessary for most religious believers when they do or don't support someone who is gay, knowing that this in itself will have the potential to invite controversy with some people. But comprehending why those who believe in religion are concerned with how others live is more complex than we might expect, as well as understanding why they may expect others to be different than they are. Most are held captive by their beliefs and have no resources available that could help or change their way of thinking.

The religious people that I've met over the years all have the same views on homosexuality—that it is a sin—but they all deal with it differently. Most of their views about homosexuality are limited to what they have been taught, although today this has dramatically changed. Most people I know now has someone related to them or someone they know who is gay. Despite this, most of our beliefs in religion have not changed. It's an indication that most have chosen to be silent. I'm not sure if we could consider this as our pretending to act as if we accept someone for whom they are when we actually are against them or their beliefs. I think that this is the way most religious people naturally react without thought. We try to seem as if we understand people, and we act as if we can relate to who they are. No matter what you say about your life that is against their beliefs, most will act as if they understand you. They will give you a smile, a hug, and the right conversation about your life, but they actually are totally against you and your way of life or lifestyle. I'm not sure if this is done purposely or if it's just a genuine way that most of us act. But it does however expose what some religious believers actually think and do.

There are some religions that may be more aggressive in their belief against homosexuality or anything that they consider a violation of their belief. Of course, their way of thinking is more extreme than most other religious beliefs, and also is their tolerance for it. Those religions that are extreme in their belief will expel anyone for homosexuality or for anything else they consider as immoral. Their reason for this is usually justified by the thought that they are building members who are pure and that all their members have good morals. It's as if they believe that their belief is actually God's law for us, and it requires us to not associate with certain people outside of their religion. The purpose for this behavior is that the believers feel that they are under less deception and will obtain a greater relationship with God. In fact, they would treat anyone or anything foreign to them as if it was a disease that would spread. This is evidence of how most are influenced and pressured into a belief because of their religion. Also, this gives clarity why these types of religious believers are concerned with how others live.

There are others that I have met that believe in religion but have other reasons for the way they rationalize their thinking against homosexuality. Because of their belief, most are confined by its teaching against homosexuality, but they justify their reasons for being against it differently. It's as if, for them, there is no clearly defined way of knowing how to deal with this issue the correct way. So we all uniquely interpret this and develop our own way of dealing with people. As a religious believer, most of us assume that we oppose homosexual behavior and that we are only trying to be aggressive to others who disagree with what we believe our religion is about. We think that we are expressing our commitment to what we believe in. In fact, most believe that we are honoring God by correcting others with our belief. I believe that most religious believers stand for what they are taught, and their pursuit to correct others is out of their sincerity of what they think is a benefit to those who they are advising. In fact, this type of religious believer will seem as if they support homosexuality and those who advocate for its equality, although if they are cornered with no way out, they will eventually reveal their hatred for it. It's as if they either don't feel comfortable to take a position on this issue, or they don't want to risk having an unpopular point of view. They will fundamentally be against homosexuality, but they will publicly support the equality of it. They are actually leaders of religion who teach and preach the message of unity with its members, convincing everyone that they must accept all those who come to worship as they are and that they accept worshiping with gay people as part of their belief. This happens within certain religions.

Actually there are certain religious institutions that are against judging or condemning others for what they do, and in fact, some think that their mission would be counterproductive if they treated people without compassion despite what the laws are for their religion. Their contact with people is on a humanity basis without concern for their way of life. Their belief is that their way of helping others will result in transforming the lives of people. After they have experienced such compassion from a stranger, I believe that most religious people that believe as they do avoid having thoughts of condemnation of others. It's not as if their religious beliefs support the cause of homosexuality equality, but that their focus is on a mission of compassion to help others. Ultimately, their concern is nonjudgmental, and they expect nothing in return for what they do. Their reason for being concerned for the way people live their lives is the example that we can all learn from. Despite this, there are some people that will continue to be hurtful and disrespectful when they oppose one's views. However, it's important to know that when this happens, most do so with the thinking that others don't rise to their level of spirituality.

Ultimately, they act as if they are a divine entity representing God for others to follow. I'm not sure if some people are conscious of how they appear to others when they are doing this. It's as if they're under a deceptive spirit to feel that they are closer to God than everyone else. I think that some act as if religion has been a type of investment for them that they begin to claim ownership of certain aspects from the institutions they are involved with. Religious believers' reasons for being concerned with how others live are not limited to those outside the church but also inside its institutions of belief. The diversity of all our religions is a direct example of the way religion has divided itself over the differences of the way we think others should live their lives that are part of its body of believers. This is a time when being an individual with a religious belief that is different from someone else's that we potentially can be attacked by others because of what we think. Our differences over how we interpret the Scriptures or how we worship God differently gives a reason for some to behave this way.

There are some that will argue over the importance of our Bible's Old Testament and say that it is more relevant than the New Testament. But I think both are just as relevant, and having one without the other would be telling an incomplete story. However, this is an example of how our religion has expectations of those who follow. It can be confusing to understand why most experienced followers and leaders of various religions do not realize that around their network of religious leaders is this: A relationship that pretends to love exists within most; but also just as quick to condemn. Most are easily intimidated by the leadership of others that overshadows their success, and a majority have a complex of other leaders having more followers than they have. It's as if the more followers they have, represents their status of power, or their intellectual superiority in religion. It's a clear sign to other leaders of their success or failure to lead people more effectively than they can. Once we understand that it's our religious beliefs that are sometimes our worst critics. We come to realization of these facts, which should be a sobering thought for some. It represents the fact that religious condemnation has no barriers or respecter of persons. Its hatred and condemnation reaches within, as well as outside of its institutions.

The inexperienced followers that come to worship usually don't discover the "behind-the-scenes" drama that occurs within the leadership of the church they attend. If this were possible, it could reveal the inner thinking of hidden feelings of most people that they wouldn't normally share with others. Actually, we would learn just how human everyone is. Essentially, religious followers have different reasons for why they are concerned with how others live their lives. From this, we understand that this practice is within its own body of believers as well. I think that this represents a larger picture of what's happening with things that we don't see on the surface or realize that we actually ignore it in some way. We are all concerned in different ways with how others live their lives. We may never have thought to question the fact as to why so many of us are so concerned with what others do or don't do. Without this analytical view, we would seem less concerned as a society about what our citizens do. If we could imagine a world in which everyone in it had no concern with how others live and if our society was not designed with the thought of concern for how others lived their lives, there would be no need for many of the things that are designed just for those that we are concerned about. For example, we have many different devices that assist handicapped people to overcome their challenges, which is a direct result from someone concerned for the way they lived their lives. We design our society around our needs. In other words, we are designed as a society specifically to assist everyone with how they live their lives.

As a society, we are concerned with how our children learn or what they eat. We have established a society full of guidelines from our concern. Our institutions for how others live life is an example of our humanitarian efforts that we establish out of concern for how other live. In fact, our entire social order is out of concern for how we live, beginning with the traffic lights that control where we go and when as well as our laws that enforce what we are allowed to do so that others are protected. Basically our laws in society are established with the sole purpose of concern for how we live our lives. Most of society tells us when it is safe to travel and what route to take for our safety. Our society has guidelines for how we raise our children and what foods we eat. Nutritional guidelines and recommended living tips by experts continue to influence what we eat and drink and how we should exercise.

Our concern for how others live has evolved to the need for some to help with how to make decisions in our marriage, or for the need of management of our money. Basically what I'm trying to demonstrate is how everyone has a different concern and reason for how we live our lives, whether they are laws or individuals who profit from their services for our benefit. Essentially, despite the many different examples, we all have a reason to justify our concern for how others live. Our society has established its social order on the very basis of concern for how we live our lives. It anticipates things that we need and establishes laws to enforce it. Understanding what drives our interest when we are concerned with how others live is something most may have never considered as being important or worth their time to do. Most likely, we may have never considered just how we are affected by those around us, even with the people that we don't know.

Essentially, everyone has an idea of what we dislike in some people. We may not be able to explain why we think or feel the way we do or be able to articulate to others what bothers us about them. Although, we are fully aware of how we feel about people, sometimes it may seem as if we can't control what we think. We have an impulse to react to what we feel is odd or out of place. We look at others and analyze the way they live their lives, and we ether encourage, discourage, or determine its value. For most of us, the reason why we are concerned with how others live is because of an innocent desire to understand or correct something that is different. Everyone may have people who are closely connected to them that they have expectations of in the way they live their lives. It could be as simple as a child who came home with a tattoo that upset their parents, or the parent who showed up intoxicated at a school function that embarrassed a child. Despite our reasons for why we are concerned with how others live, it is usually something more explainable that exists within us that we cannot intelligently explain. We are driven by what we feel or what we expect out of others, even those we have never met. I actually believe that most people who are concerned with the way others live justify how they think by the way they feel about things, despite the circumstances. In fact, there may be many different examples of the way parents may have expectations of their children or many different examples of children being rebellious to their parents. Because of their children's expectations, this could be used as an example in revealing why most are concerned with how others live whether they are or are not in a close relationship.

If we were to use these two incidents as our example, we would realize how the child who is embarrassed over the parent reflects what kind of concern and why. Essentially, this child is concerned about what others think of their parents. It is as if they are protecting their integrity by hiding their parent's dysfunction from others. There can be many different examples of why children begin to think this way, but from this example, what can be learned is that we all have a reason why certain people live their lives the way they do. It seems that this is proof that children actually expect for their parents to behave a certain way. This demonstrates why children are concerned about the way their parents present themselves to others that they know. Our children are concerned with the method that their parents use, that form from the basis for their opinions. They often complain that parents cannot relate to their life or their experiences. Often, some act as if their parents are newly created and uninformed of what is going on in this world. Some children feel that that their parents' ideas are obsolete and that they have an outdated way of thinking. It is as if their parents can no longer act in the capacity of one worthy to lead others with their advice.

As a child, I remember how I felt when my mother came to my school and how I was embarrassed over the wig she wore when her hair wasn't presentable. I actually thought that her wig was worse than her unpresentable hair. I felt embarrassed by the way she presented herself. My concern was influenced by what I thought my school friends would say. My mom's lack of education was noticeable by me when she could not help me with simple homework. Because of this, I became concerned with the possibility that this would be revealed to people and would be a source of ridicule for my schoolmates. Also, I felt that her lack of education would be noticed not just by students but also by my teachers. But what I felt about my mother and her education did not stop me from being appreciative for her love and affection for me. My love for her and my concern for way she lived her life was a totally separate issue. Actually, my concern with the way she lived her life had more to do with my issues than hers. The facts become more transparent that this was about the way I felt, based upon what others thought about me and my mom. I wanted my mom to be seen by others differently so that they would see me in a unique way.

Nevertheless, understanding why the parent is troubled over their children when they come home with a tattoo is an issue that most kids don't appreciate or even comprehend. As a parent, I experienced this with some of my children. In the beginning I felt exactly the same way, although every parent may have different reasons for what they feel about their child's choice to wear tattoos or even body piercings. Despite this, it's important to understand why they think this way. At the time, I felt that it was something that could get in their way of finding a good job or a spouse, or that it makes them appear as if they are a street person. Having a tattoo to me represented someone hardcore with a rebellious attitude or a person that spoke their mind to others quickly. It seemed to me as if it was something negatively associated with my children having a tattoo, and I could not articulate how I felt to them in words.

Despite our love or how closely associated we are with people, our concern will remain the way we feel others should live their lives. It's important to note that this happens with most, and that these are usually people that we actually care for. My children did not look at their body display as being what I thought it was but as art on display. It was clear to me that my objection to their body tattoos was my personal opinion without a legitimate reason to them for having it. I could not claim that it has caused any direct harm to me other than what others that knew me may think, and this was my only reason. I mean, this was the reason that bothered me most—what everyone would think about them over their tattoos. Another major reason could be because of the way I always thought about people with tattoos before my children were conceived. It was something that I thought was strange, and I never understood why anyone would like having something permanent on their bodies. I felt that my children and their decision to get a tattoo was a spontaneous event that took place, which led to their addiction of wanting to have more tattoos. Their tattoos are but a few of the things in our children's lives that we are concerned about. What is important is that we learn that our concern is not a factor to them but a distraction. This is when our children will begin to question why their parents are so concerned with how they live their lives.

Our expectations for the way others live their lives can be strange to understand. For example, I have children and other relatives who married outside of their race. This is not something that is unusual, though every time I get new information of another relative doing this, I still have a negative response when I learn about it. Overtime, it began to be more obvious to me why I felt this way. After I privately analyzed the reasons for my thoughts, it almost made no sense to me at first, being that there were already several members of my family that were of different nationalities. When I discovered someone else that was biracial and it bothered me, this became a reason for my concern. I had to better understand why I was bothered by relatives when I first found out that they were attracted to someone they had met that was outside of our ethnic group. Even though I felt bothered by it after discovering this, eventually I would find a way to overcome how I felt. As I sought to better understand it, I discovered certain things about why I thought this way. It somehow was strange to me that I cared so much about their choice of who they chose to be with. I had to reason with myself and had to slow down my thoughts and rationalize what was happening. That was when the reality of my bigotry began to bother me. There was no escape for me.

At this point, I began to reason with myself as to why I felt this way. From this, I was able to face the facts of my selfishness. This is the period when we all discover ourselves, or at least a part of ourselves. This is also when I had to surrender to the reality that I was wrong for thinking or feeling this way. It felt like this process of admitting that we are wrong was one of the hardest things to accept at first. When faced with this, we might search for every possible justification for our bigotry of others, but we continue coming up with a weak defense. We are never willing to accept being wrong as the way to solve what we are dealing with. However, for me to resolve my issues with relatives who did affect me, this process was necessary. When I reasoned with myself, it was necessary to ask myself what I would think if I were in that situation. Most importantly, I had to be truthful with myself in admitting that the way I felt was a wrong way to feel.

Experience has taught me that it is better to deal with our pain and face it head on rather then let it bother us. I believe that by doing this, we save ourselves from going through a more intensive process of dysfunction in our lives and within our families. It can be an experience similar to when we are trying to overcome any bad habits of ours. The first important thing is for us to be aware of what our defects are and admit it and then to begin to deal with our process to heal. We literally need to reshape our thoughts and emotions about our bigotry. We need to have a reason for this. It cannot be a conversion that is only to impress others; it should be a genuine attempt to overcome what we have already concluded is wrong. This method has to be an intentional, well-thought-out process for us to overcome what we feel. Essentially, we must change by realizing our defects. Our learning must come from our evidence of facts and not from the persuasion of others for us to change. This process helped me understand why I was so concerned for how others that were related to me who dated others outside their own race, and this became the instrument that helped me to overcome. Of course, this process doesn't happen overnight. Overcoming our hatred and emotions is a development that requires us to be aware at all times that it is wrong to be this way. We must go to battle with our thoughts. We do this by refusing to accept what we know is wrong. Understanding my hatred and that I had no foundation to stand on made me realize that there was this person that was a part of me that had victimized other people. This actually revealed my dark side, and it was something that I did not like about myself. But in the end, it helped and motivated me to change.

This experience made me question other aspects of my hatred and discomfort for other people and the way they lived their lives. I think that we all have many different types of people who have beliefs and lifestyles that we fundamentally disagree with. Of course, we try to be polite and appear to others as if we understand their perspectives about why they live their life a certain way. But we never face the reality of our opposition and why we feel the way we do. We don't want others to know how we actually feel about them. My sisters are a good example for me because of my relationship with having homosexuality as something I had to face with them. I learned some essential aspects about my behavior with this experience, but the most difficult part of it all was understanding *why* I was so concerned with the way they lived their lives. I had no difficulty in feeling as if I was against them and everyone else for what they believed, but it was difficult for me to explain exactly why. I felt that my way of life was the only way for anyone. It wasn't as if anything was thought out in detail about their homosexuality as much as it was just my being opposed to it. Of course, I would come up with my reasons, but most would be justified by the normal things, such as religion. I felt that in order for my thoughts about this to be more legitimate, I needed to go beyond the normal excuses that people used, which was religion. That was when I became stuck, and I couldn't move forward. I struggled to express what

I deeply felt within me, but words could not express what I felt about their homosexuality.

Factually speaking, everything I said in opposition to my sisters and their life actually ended up being an instrument of hurt for all of us. I began to realize that when I hurt others, it hurt me as well. I realized that no one can obtain inner satisfaction at the expense of someone's hurt and pain. My intellectual way of looking at it was confusing me, but it allowed me to overcome my feelings. This was the breakthrough for me when I put aside how I felt and when I began to realize that this was not all about me and what I thought. In fact, if we were facing a certain situation that was potentially life-threatening, most of us would think differently about the world that we are about to leave behind. We would face the reality of how insignificant our opinions will soon be after we leave this earth. When I begin to transform my thoughts based on this reality, it was easier to do. What I mean is that I was able to relate better. I began to understand that my presence on this earth is just a journey, and in this journey, we will see many things that we like and don't like. Whether we agree or disagree with them, the world will eventually do what it will despite what we think. Essentially, I had to accept the fact that my hatred for others would not change the world or the things that I hated about a person. It only seemed to have affected me, the one who held hatred of others over their life choices. When I compared my hatred response to one of compassion and love, there was no way to compare the differences of the two. Having compassion and love definitely empowers a person. When our tool of love is used instead of hatred, we benefit.

There are several ways we benefit from doing this, and it starts with the reality that we know we are doing our best by having compassion instead of hatred for someone. We are able to feel certain about ourselves no matter what the outcome is. When we exercise our love and compassion instead of our hatred, it is something that is always noticed by the recipient of it. It usually brings harmony to our relationships instead of strife. When we do this, we no longer are "the accuser of our brethren." We learn to accept others based upon something more important than what we think or feel. Learning the right way to treat others that we oppose should be our goal in the things that we seek with the people that we oppose. My compassion and love for others are the only things that I pursued that made progress to my sanity. My sisters' homosexuality had a more deeply rooted hold on me that made me see things differently and was more difficult for me. It had nothing to do with the measure of my love that guided my feelings, but with my morals and beliefs of things that I could not properly articulate and which I believed to be the guideline for all of us.

Despite the way I felt about my sisters' homosexuality, my goal was to maintain our relationships. I was successful in maintaining a relationship with one of my sisters, but not with the other. I started to remember before all of this began how I felt and that my problem with my youngest sister's homosexuality had a lot to do with our failure for us to continue to be closer with each other. However, for me to find a resolution to this issue, it was necessary for me to look at the situation with my sisters' homosexuality from a different perspective. The first way of doing this was to understand that I was not solely the one who created this confusion, but that I was seeking the right method to deal with it. Based upon that principle by itself, is a self-admission to being powerless to have control over what people do; even if it is someone close to us. Ultimately, our love can be used as a tool by some to go against others and their freedom of choice, or hopefully could be used as an anchor of trust for them to depend on. Most religious believers are uneducated in the subject of homosexuality and lack the social skills in being able to accept or to change someone that is opposed to our traditions and beliefs.

I must admit, however, that my sisters' homosexuality was a different challenge to my relationship than anything else that

I experienced with them. It was difficult then and now for me to completely understand or always properly react to certain elements of it. When I first discovered the knowledge of their homosexuality, it was difficult at first to accept the reality of it. Nonetheless, as time passed, it became a matter of learning and adjusting to the changes and challenges that opposed my belief. The problem most may have when accepting someone's homosexuality is the attempt to not be contradicting in their beliefs or traditions of religion, as we do when we accept someone's homosexuality, or so we think. For some reason, we feel that we must agree with others and their beliefs as a requirement for us to have compassion for them. Learning this fundamental principle was important; but what was more vital was later balancing what I felt inside so that I wasn't unfair in my thoughts about my sisters' homosexuality. It was necessary to set aside my pride to patronize her point of view, knowing that I was really trying to adapt to the way they thought without causing hurt to them. However, trying to accept something that you fundamentally have always opposed was not simple for most to do, and it is partly the blame for most of our issues that divides our society today. In fact, many may not think that they should change their thinking; rather, they think others should instead.

I suppose it doesn't make a difference if we are concerned with how someone lives because of interracial dating, homosexual dating, or the many other reasons for others and their choices for how they live that bothers us. Ultimately, who are we to judge anyway? Homosexuals and their voices should be heard as well as those that oppose it. We need to understand that we don't control others and their freedom of thought or the way they wish to live. Our challenge should be in the way we adapt to others without requiring people to live by our expectations. To accomplish this, it is helpful to remind ourselves that we are only passing through this life, and our judgment and what we expect of others is temporary. This world will evolve despite our opinions. If we could realize that our attempt to change others with our hatred is what divides us, then maybe we are left with the only thing left to persuade others that no one opposes, which is when we have compassion and consideration for others and their views. This power of compassion for others is something that we are all capable of possessing. It is the thing that we all should be able to relate to the most and as something we are all capable of as well.

I believe that the reason why most are concerned with how others live is because they struggle to understand why people do things that are against their values and beliefs. Or maybe they think that their belief is untrue and difficult for most to accept. We all have a need to be accepted for what we believe, and most of us want others to acknowledge what is sacred to us. The only thing that is certain about our life is when our death will bring about our silence with everyone living in this world. Despite what we do or have done, life will continue to evolve hereafter. We eventually realize that we don't control the voice of God's creation nor are we the enforcer to change everyone we know that differ with us in our views. Our ability to adapt to the diversity of everyone should be the example for others, and our compassion to accept those that are different from us should be a guideline for everyone to follow. As of today, there is no road map we can clearly follow other than our refusal to condemn others with our hatred. We should uplift those instead with our patience and compassion for who they are or choose to be.

9

Torn Between My Love for God and Gays Summary and Conclusion

Being torn between our religion and homosexuality is when we feel that despite what we believe regarding homosexuality, our decisions to accept others that are homosexuals will conflict with our religious belief. This happens also when we add up all our reasons to justify our religious condemnation of others, but we keep coming up short of proving our case. Our logic and reasoning for our religious belief that we once thought of as being built on a solid foundation, we feel is now fragile, and others have been able to poke holes and caused confusion in our point of view.

At this time, it may become more difficult for us to face others in any debate about their homosexuality, even if we feel that we can justify everything with our religious belief. When we are torn between our God and the homosexuality of others is when with our good intentions, we are trying to enforce our belief on others. We eventually came to the realization that when we are torn between our belief and those who are homosexual, we are actually trusting in our views through the belief system of our religious traditions. The fact is that doing this serves as our biggest hurdle when finding solutions that can bring harmony for us on this issue.

Being torn between homosexuality and religion is when we are trying to accept the homosexuality of those we know, and while doing this, we somehow develop a guilty feeling about our religion and of how it judges homosexuals. We have no good explanation to give in response to others that disagree with the Bible regarding God's commandments about homosexuality. While trying to express our views, most times we don't want others to feel as if we are personally putting them down or trying to imply that they themselves as homosexuals are living against God's law for mankind. However, eventually, we discover that our message about God is harder to explain when the subject we are debating on is homosexuality. When we're at this stage, this is an obvious sign of how we are in the midst of a struggle with our belief in religion, which is competing for the understanding of homosexuality with those that we know and love. This also happens when we do not maintain relationships with those that are not living by our religion and traditions. Instead of trying to solve our problems with others, some of us choose to do nothing when faced with this. We feel as if our advice to others won't change anything, or it could be from our past experience of when we do voice our opinion about anything related to religion that this in the past in itself has caused a problem in our relationship with others. Although, we will later confirm that when we are discussing homosexuality with others, that this may be risky and may not be the best way for someone to create change in others.

I feel that my situation is not unique in how I view homosexuality and religion. I know now that there are many others that dislike how the religious community has dealt with homosexuality. Although, some of those that do seem to ignore that they are guilty of treating gays as if they are not worthy of our religion. When this happens, we all could be considered torn between the conflicts that exist between those who believe in our religious traditions that are straight and those who believe in religion that are homosexual.

Being torn between our religion and homosexuality is when we attempt to act as if we are *for* homosexuality equality, when actually we are not. Most of us either lack having the facts to defend their belief of being against homosexuality, or they lack facts to support justifying the reasons why their religious views are that way. We also lack having the facts that motivates others to agree in what we believe. Most of us think we know why God is against homosexuality, but we really can't locate the exact scriptures proving this. The reason for this is because often we have been taught this way of measuring others by our religion and oftentimes, we did not investigate the facts of biblical scriptures for ourselves. Most of us have assumed that what we are told by our religious leaders are always factual. Although, when we are torn between our religion and homosexuality, we sometimes cannot clearly verbalize why we believe homosexuality is wrong and why God is against it. Typically, most of us don't exactly know what God's entire commandments are for us. It seems that a majority of us can be satisfied with what we are taught by our religious leaders, and most of the time we do this with our blind trust. In fact, the majority of us defend our religious beliefs and traditions without knowing all the facts.

There are homosexuals who are torn between wanting to love or rebel against our belief in religion and its followers, partly because religious believers have not recognized their desire of wanting to love God and to have a God for their salvation equally as others. It seems that for homosexuals, trying to love God can be a challenge for most within our institutions. Some may feel that God may not equally love them, which is what has always been rumored by those who make false claims. But this myth has not been proven to be factual as God's actual way of thinking. However, God's actual intent is that everyone will be accepted equally the same as others that seek God has been altered by some that would like it to appear that religion is off-limits to certain people as a consequence of their homosexuality and other violations of belief. Because of our religious traditions, many of our religious leaders and believers feel that those living in a homosexual relationship are not qualified for God's grace because of what they believe. They have decided that His commandments for us to love all others somehow did not include those who are homosexuals. This also demonstrates how homosexuals may often feel torn between themselves and their belief of God as compared to those who are straight. It further proves that being torn between God and gays does affect homosexuals as well as those that are not, causing us all in being torn between God and all our different beliefs.

It's unfair that in order for homosexuals to be accepted as others are, that there are conditions required by certain religious believers. They act as if homosexuals are expected to change first before they are eligible for grace and forgiveness. It's almost as if they must prequalify first for God's love. It may be that some homosexuals may actually feel torn between whether it is worth their effort to seek God for their salvation or not, because of what others in the religious world say. Maybe because of this, they are not as certain as most that God's grace will be for them as it is for others. They may feel torn between wanting to seek God and the fear that they will not be accepted by those in the religious community. They may conclude because of this, that despite what they do, that most religious views have already labeled them as sinful and beyond their ability to help. They must overcome significant pressures to change themselves first, that most others don't ever have to deal with. There are many other significant issues that may cause homosexuals to be torn between themselves, their beliefs, and God. Often, others that are straight and who claim to know God do not understand what homosexuals may actually feel and think.

One of the major obstacles for homosexuals to overcome in getting equality from religion is: How they must be *torn between* believing whether they really are loved by others in the religious community or not. I feel that our religious leaders and followers have not brought enough clarity to this point. We have not been effective as a religious institution of convincing homosexuals that we love them as we love ourselves, as an example of what God expects of us. We seem to fall short of living up to God's requirement for how we are expected to love others, and because of this, we cannot find fault with those who are homosexuals that make this type of claim about us having religious intolerance for their homosexuality. Also, this further demonstrates our religious leaders' lack of ability to lead with authority on the subject of homosexuality. When our leaders and ministers are torn between God and homosexuality, it's actually better demonstrated when their message to others is filled with extreme hatred of homosexuality, followed by saying why they are going to hell for their belief. This is an example of when their leadership is based upon what God will do in their opinion on judgment day, instead of focusing on what can be done today to prevent someone from disappointing God while there still remains time. Another example of how our leaders are torn between God and homosexuality is when they often try to use their acts of God's judgment on others because of their beliefs and religious traditions, instead of showing compassion despite someone's differences.

When our leaders are torn between God and homosexuality, it can be very noticeable by others, just with the way our religious leaders teach on the issue of homosexuality within itself can reveal whether they feel secure with their belief in God and his requirements of us as it relates to the homosexuality of others. Their message can encourage homosexuals to become closer to religion or push them further away from this belief by the way God is represented, especially to those that have not understood religion before. Some of our religious leaders' messages about homosexuality or about God do not have the necessary sensitivity that demonstrates that this spiritual experience is also for those who are homosexual. In short, it seems that most of the time, our leaders' biblical teachings regarding homosexuality appears that its focus is more directed on teaching others about how and why they will go to hell, more so than explaining how and why homosexuals need and deserve heaven and the greater things from God as others do. However, as believers and followers of our religion, we have also become torn between our religion and homosexuality. Most religious followers are torn between the message that they're taught: of tolerance or intolerance for homosexuality. The message that we are taught can be contradictory in itself, because it teaches us to love all people but also encourages those who believe in religion and God to sometimes take on the false belief that they deserve to feel and act superior to those who don't believe as they do. It appears that most believers of religion actually never become as encouraged to help homosexuals as they do with others. It seems that most of us who believe in God act as if we may become dirty if we associate with homosexuals or anyone that don't appear to be part of our religious traditions and beliefs. We have established certain conditions and expectations that we feel others should live by before we are willing to feel comfortable with them.

Most followers of religion that are torn between God and homosexuality are this way because they lack the knowledge of how to represent themselves in the way God actually intended them to do. Our religious focus is usually on us and our desires, instead of it being on others and their spiritual needs. It is as if we are disturbed around others that are not as we are when it comes to our religious or personal beliefs. We are torn with God's directive when we do this, which is "to love others as we love ourselves." The fact that our religion has taught us that God hates certain things about what mankind does has been used as a method of deception to deceive others about homosexuality, as if it were a slam-dunk case that all homosexuals were bound for hell and as if this judgment by God was just for homosexuals and not others. This type of thinking by some of our religious followers attempts to imply that the promise by God of His forgiveness and grace are excluded from those that are gay, and some people are trying to say that God really did not consider homosexuals to be part of his plan for salvation. By this, it's obvious that we are often torn by what we think God's expectation for us should or should not be; even though later we may discover that most times God's purpose for us is to learn to love those that we dislike as a lesson for us in our outreach while we are helping others. When we disregard others and their needs because of our selfish or prejudiced way of thinking, we miss the lesson that otherwise we would have learned from that experience. Often, we are torn between wanting to live the right way that God tells us and trying to do it without homosexuals involved in our lives, even though our mission from God is for us to help all who need God.

Our lack of clarity of what God expects of us is often what has led to our mistakes. One example is this: As followers of our religious belief, how we are often torn between God and homosexuality as a result of having homosexuality in our family or with those that we know and love. When it is our family, often it becomes personal for us and sometimes becomes our barrier of whether we're accepting homosexuality or not with those we love and know. As followers of God, our responsibility to treat others in a godly manner will be tested when this happens to us. It can feel as if we are torn between what we believe in religion and our opinions or what we think about of others. We all respond to this differently. We can become insensitive in the way we treat those that don't believe the same as we do. We feel as followers of God, that we have a special privilege with Him. Sometimes we seek to stand out as everyone's example of how to live right by God. Most of those who claim to be followers of God do not recognize their lack of love to those that we don't like or that it is our requirement by God to care for others that are different from us.

Being followers of our religious beliefs and having a lack of education about our belief have led to our uncertainty about God. Sometimes this can be a stumbling block that stops us from realizing our actual moral principles that our religion expects of us as well as God's required expectations for us. When we, as followers of our religion, are torn between our religious beliefs and homosexuality, we cannot intelligently explain our religious beliefs to others without our emotions taking over. When we are torn this way, we often cannot explain our feelings or rationalize why we are defending our belief. It seems that we are torn between knowing how to verbalize what we feel because we lack the sufficient arsenal of evidence to support our belief. It begins to feel for us that our religious views are actually our personal views gone wrong. Our confusion over this subject is proof of our lack of knowledge about religion and our religious traditions. When we as believers of God are torn between our belief and homosexuality because of not knowing what to say to homosexuals. In the process of doing this, it is amazing to realize how we are so focused on their homosexuality, as the main issue of what's wrong and that we're so busy analyzing their life and how they appear to us that our words might sometimes escape us. It seems that developing a relationship with gays may be difficult for some of us partly because we think that homosexuals cannot relate to our same experiences or because they are so different.

Often, we don't want to be seen by the public when we are with someone we know or care for that is homosexual and dresses in a way that others can still notice their gender. Frequently, we consider our outreach of love for them to be good enough. We may feel that being around them when everyone else knows their gay might be embarrassing and asking too much of us. We act as if we don't have enough confidence to face others in regard to their homosexuality, and most times we don't bother to explain what we want to say because we feel that it would expose how we actually think about their homosexuality; at least, this is how it was for me.

As a believer of religion I found myself torn between my religious belief and the issue of homosexuality, partly because my religion has always been my foundation for the way I measure everything including homosexuality, although for me, my sisters served as a way to help neutralize my disrespect for gays. My feeling was that I did not create religion or our religious traditions, and nor am I responsible for people's life choices. In fact, sometimes I think that I am forced to have an opinion because I'm a citizen of this world or because I'm a human. I think because of our religion, and everyone explaining to others how we should live and act in our society, and particularly the traditions of our religion, as a result, this has made me think that now I'm in conflict with homosexuals that are fighting for their equality; because of this, I feel that trying to live as an example of what I believe in God, just got a lot harder for me. It has challenged me and everyone else that believe in God to take inventory of themselves differently than before and respond to homosexuality. We all at some point have to make critical choices that will affect our relationships with not only those we know, but also with our belief in doing what's right as well. I believe most of us that believe in religion might hesitate before starting a conversation on the subject of homosexuality. It's obvious that it is too confusing and controversial for most of us. We feel that remaining neutral is a nonaggressive way to approach those we know with the subject of homosexuality and religion without our true feelings being known. It can feel by some believers as if it is our white flag of surrender to the pressures of debating our differences in religion with those who are gay advocates.

As I evolved in my thinking with my sisters and their homosexuality, a part of me felt as if I had surrendered to this way of thinking with them and their way of life. It felt that my religion was seen by them as a potential threat to their quality of their homosexuality, and it became obvious that it wasn't the appropriate conversation for me to talk about when they were around. I could not find my comfort zone when discussing religion with them. Also, I did not feel that it would be received by them or other homosexuals in the way I intended, and it might lead to me being accused of having religious condemnation of others, just because of my belief in God. Throughout all my years of going to church, I had only met maybe one or two people that I confirmed was homosexual who was a member of our church. Although if there were others I did not know it. But just the mere fact that I've only met a few homosexuals in all my fifty-plus years of going to church proves that there is a disconnect with gays and religion. Nevertheless, as I reflect back, I see how this may have affected my feelings for how I viewed my sisters Now I actually feel that I only just evolved. I also realize that I responded in two different ways with them, and I received two different responses in the way they responded back to me. One way was good, and the other was not so good, but I also gained valuable information that will help me relate to this differently in the future, and hopefully my readers will as well.

One of these challenges for me was accepting that my world was changing, and there was nothing I could do to stop it. I felt that homosexuality was now accepted more by society than ever before. In fact on July 29, 2013, **Pope Francis** was the first pope to say, "People should not be marginalized," when talking to media on an airplane that day. He also is quoted by the media as saying, "If a person is gay and seeks God and has good will, who am I to judge him"? This is probably the first time that one of our most respected religions had a religious leader that has taken this type of position on homosexuality, and this serves as proof that our religious values are in competition with the values of those who advocate for homosexual equality against our religious traditions and beliefs. I'm personally hoping for equality for homosexuals in their pursuit to seek God, and I hope that our religions around the world can learn to lead with love and avoid going against what God has commanded of us. I felt that because of my journey of life and in the way I dealt with homosexuals, that it was necessary for me to know the borders that confine me in the decisions that I make. In order to comprehend this better, it was important for me to start with the basic human instincts of love and kindness, which fundamentally is one of the main conditions that God requires of us.

As religious believers, our religion and faith in God requires us to go through different conflicts because of us being in direct opposition with others and their beliefs, whether we realize it or not. For me, understanding that this has happened in the past and is illustrated in many different well-noted biblical events and that it still exists with others today over homosexuality demonstrated that this is only one aspect of change that is needed, giving reasons as to why many people in our world will continue to pursue homosexual equality in all segments of our society. Although for many of us to adapt to this change, it will require all of us as religious believers to adapt or to change, or eventually be excluded from our new society formed out of the purpose pursued for homosexual equality. Because of the effect of this change, I believe it is no doubt that this will make religion less appealing or more threatening to others. It will be seen as if it harms the fabric of our society by some, and because of further homosexuality equality breakthroughs, we as religious believers must expect more challenges to come that will threaten the purpose and intent of our religious traditions that is in the future, the parts that are negatively effecting homosexuality. I believe these things will eventually happen everywhere we go.

At times, to me it seems that I am still evolving in my way of looking at homosexuality. It's not as if I have a choice; rather, it's a reflection of the many different ways that our society is changing. As we are adjusting ourselves to homosexuality as I have done, something new is always discovered that we should change in what we do, and sometimes we must adjust how we feel about things to completely get there. I had to change my belief about how I originally felt about homosexuals wanting to have equality, especially in having their God-given choice to live how they wish. I was influenced by the fact that God himself allows mankind to make our independent choices about how we want to live, and the fact that God has never forced any one of us to accept a certain way to live, rather has only put into place a road map to get to Him and has highlighted the areas of our map that is off-limits. Despite this, God still allows us the choice to choose and allows us to have freedom of choice in everything that we choose to do. He has warned us, similar to what happened to Adam and Eve in the Garden of Eden, who were warned not to eat of the forbidden fruit. Although, God still allowed Adam and Eve the freedom to choose, He did not try to hide the forbidden fruit from them; but God like He does with us, actually allowed them their freedom of choice. I feel that homosexuals deserve freedom of choice not necessarily because of right or wrong views as my point, but rather that God designed it to be this way and anyone who changes this process does so at great risk of being guilty of changing what He has designed for everyone.

Besides, our efforts to change the world from homosexuality with our religious beliefs may be what we hope, but it is not likely to happen—especially considering what recent history has demonstrated with all the homosexual equality advances in our world. I eventually began to believe that the institution of God is now at a point in time that it has not ever been before. Not only is it just me and my family that I was dealing with, but now it's my religion itself that is dealing with homosexuality with its priests. For example, on July 29, 2013, **Pope Francis's** answer on homosexuality was also directed at its gay Catholic priests as well as the world of homosexuality. It appears that this serves as direct evidence that our religion is also torn between homosexuality within itself and that religion as a whole is in direct conflict with the world's changing opinion over accepting homosexuality. For me, this also serves as evidence how homosexual advances continue to conflict with our religious traditions and beliefs. However, at this point, it's hard to measure how it will change over time, but it's safe to say that our society will change.

My change in thought about religious condemnation came when I started feeling as the Pope felt, and that is, "Who am I to judge?" I really feel that whether we agree or not with this pope and his opinion, that despite what we think it seems as though it is in line with what God expects of us. Also, I felt that my former opinion of others who are gay was insulting to them and is what hindered me from having complete happiness. It was weird to me to see how my negative opinions about others can actually result in me experiencing that same negative energy. Although, what's weird is how replacing it with my positive energy could actually be my way of obtaining inner joy. Now, I have decided from experience that having positive opinions of others most of the time creates positive responses from them, and I've learned that it is not my responsibility to correct or judge others. In fact, I've also learned judging others creates stress and depression for me and steals my joy. I have had to surrender from having religious condemnation of those that I have previously disrespected because of feelings that were driven from my beliefs. Now, I am more content with the thought that I am in control of not judging others that don't live life by my religious beliefs. Now I know that it is okay by the religious beliefs of our religion to feel this way. Now I also know that God does not want any of us to live with our guilt because of what others do, and He does not expect us to act on His behalf. In fact, when we try acting on His behalf, we are most likely considered by God as our actions being wrong. I eventually figured out that when I condemn others that it had a negative effect on me. It seemed from this that the more important way to view my religion and how it accepts homosexuality was in how we are able to adapt to our adversity. I actually feel that this is part of what we should do although knowing how to continue to pursue the love for others is not a simple task and was never an easy job for anyone to accomplish.

However, I have the belief that because of the way I've previously felt, I'm certain that my younger sister probably assumed that I was judging her indirectly on her homosexuality particularly in the way that I kept mentioning religion as if she was in violation of God. Maybe her offensive words from our past communication with each other were only meant as a warning shot to get me to not talk further about religion as if I'm advising her. Whatever it was from, she intended to communicate her anger that was directed at me, I'm certain now that I failed to respond the way I should have and the way God really requires of us. At least that was how I felt at that time.

Also, I later thought as a Christian and, most importantly, as a preacher's kid, I should have had it all together in this matter when it came to God's expectation of us. It seemed much easier for me to say that I loved others that were homosexuals as being my Christian duty than it was for me to say that about my sisters and their homosexuality. Their homosexuality was somehow actually revealing hatred within me that I did not previously admit actually existed. My problem was that this hatred I had conflicted with my deep love for my sisters and left me emotionally confused for years to come. I felt that I could not dislike them as I would if they were not my sisters. However, I could not describe the emotion of the bittersweet or love-hate type of emotions that I felt for my sisters. It took me years of simply evolving with my emotions over time.

As I tried to come to terms with the fact that my sister still had anger over what I had previously said to her, which I agreed was actually my fault, I at least felt better that I did not do the same thing with my other sister and her life partner. My other sister is the oldest, and she has a completely different personality and approach to adversity with people compared to my youngest sister. She (my older sister), her partner, and their kids have become very close to our family. Of course, this happened over a long period of time. My sister was very cautious of me and my family in the beginning. However, I'm sure that it was because they were uncertain of everyone at the time. In my earlier years of finding out about her homosexuality, I've never offered my opinion or expressed how I really felt about their lifestyle, and by doing this, I must have made it more difficult for my sisters to be certain of my support for them. However, it has become clearer to me now that one of the reasons why I did not reveal anything was because I was still evolving in my opinion of how I felt about their homosexuality. I discovered also that there were others who share these same views.

I don't think any of us respond well when we actually deal with this and it is someone we've known all of our lives. One day, you suddenly wake up and someone we know or love have changed and are now someone else. Most of us would not handle this as well as we think. Just the fact that someone we care for is now different than they were before is something that can have a powerful impact on our lives. It's not as if we carry an operational manual that informs us what to do in a situation like this. Most times, we are left with no tools at our disposal that can help guide us in knowing the best way to respond to homosexuals.

Most of us will not admit to the hatred we feel toward the homosexuality of those we know, or we might not be aware that we lack the proper education and emotional support to help us navigate through all our confusion or are aware that this prevents us from being able to have healthy relationships with gay people, and our negative opinions sometimes are hurtful to others, whether we know them or not.

I began to realize that because of my unhealthy thinking about gays, that this meant I once was torn between my religious values and my love for my sisters—which was what ultimately led to my struggle to maintain a healthy relationship with my sisters. Although later it became clearer to me that if it were not my sisters, I most likely would have not given anyone else such exceptions. I felt that with my sisters, there was a reason not to give up on our brother-sister relationship. Besides if this did not work, I concluded that they would be to blame and it would not have been because of the way I responded to them or something they did that I was angry about that offended me, which ultimately hurt our relationship. Most likely, that is how it all begins with other people as well. Most of us cannot handle the reality of it after finding out about someone's homosexuality, and usually, we are not able to stop our criticism of it, especially if it is against our religious or moral values.

I also believed, as others did, in what the Bible says, yet it seemed that this argument using religious condemnation was too difficult for me to make with my sisters. I felt very sensitive about discussing these sort of subjects with my sisters directly, yet I knew that I could not continue to ignore the fact that somehow I must deal with this and that I would be considered disingenuous to everyone connected to my family and religion if I did not. But instead, I chose to pretend as if nothing was happening. Perhaps that is what others end up doing. I think that maybe it's because of the result of the enormous and sometimes overwhelming stress that this can bring on all of us when we are faced with this type of dilemma, especially if it is someone we love and deeply care for. Our emotions can deceive us and sometimes influence our negative emotions, especially when we are just realizing the facts about their homosexuality.

Our society recently has focused on the need of our world to have homosexuality equality, but it has failed to identify the best way to motivate others how not to discriminate in their minds and hearts or how to relate this to their various religious beliefs that teach against homosexuality. We all would like to seem to others as if we have love and tolerance for everyone despite who they are, but in real life how we really and truly feel is demonstrated in how most of us are not willing to have compassion for others. In fact, often we actually don't have a position about homosexuality that we feel comfortable discussing with others, and also, we are not good at pretending to others that we are not bothered by their homosexuality when we actually are. These types of mistakes are what I was hoping to avoid with my two sisters. I did not want them to find out about the negative things that I felt about their homosexuality until I had a chance to get my thoughts under control and also until I began to be more rational in my thinking. This took time to happen for me, and trying to avoid my sisters from discovering how I truly felt has became a process to buy me more time as I was forming my opinion about homosexuality throughout the years.

My family's religious traditions and beliefs actually helped me from feeling extreme hatred for my sisters, which does not happen often enough to others in this world. Most of us cannot get over our feelings of hatred over the homosexuality in our families, even when we have religion as our foundation of belief, which requires our forgiveness and love. But with me, I felt that having hatred for anyone for any reason seemed to be the opposite of what the whole concept of religion was founded on, which is to love others and to have tolerance for others despite who they are. This is what we are taught in our religion. Sometimes we do not have a problem overlooking the small details of God requiring us to love others as being important, and I strongly believe that it is vital that we are able to discover how others bother us by what they believe. From this analysis, we should be better able to see that we do have a problem with others, especially when they are different than we are. With my sisters, I once had the temptation to use my religious condemnation as a way of proving how their homosexuality was a bad thing. But I could never get enough courage to do that. I felt that if I did something like this to them, they would think that I was being disrespectful or that I did not love them. Just the thought of doing it bothered me.

I never really felt secure with the idea that God considers this way of dealing with homosexuality to be appropriate behavior for His believers. In fact, I knew that Jesus defended the woman at the water well despite her sins and that Jesus had also demonstrated many other acts of compassion for those that were not necessarily followers or believers in religion or in God.

As I began to analyze the many different personalities of those that were homosexual, (mostly with those that I've previously met in my past and some being also from my various relatives or those that are related to them; also those I've seen on television). After this consideration, I began to feel more comfortable with my opinion about homosexuals and their different relationships. One of my first thoughts and the first things that impressed me was how most homosexuals seem to be more alive or happier than most straight people. This was followed by questioning where and how they get all this joy. I did not necessarily like people who were gay at first, although it was strange that I felt that most homosexuals were kinder to me than most other straight friends or family of mine. It seemed that their need to love and show respect for others came more naturally for them than most other people I came in contact with. Again, I was never convinced that God actually would want his followers and believers to persecute those that the Bible declares we should love. I understand that there are those in this world that will argue this point differently and feel that they should be aggressive with anyone not living by their religious standards and traditions. They will think that this is the best way to execute their God-given authority, which is to judge and penalize others.

I feel that this kind of judgmental attitude held by our religious leaders and followers is not limited to just how they feel about homosexuality. History does reflect the persecutions others suffered for these similar types of beliefs. Comparing our religion from this perspective allows all of us to see the past mistakes of mankind and of our religious institutions more clearly, and it further demonstrates how we can use that as our guideline for us to not repeat it again. In time, it became clearer to me how those that were homosexuals had qualities about them that were different than most straight people. In fact, I felt as if some of the homosexuals I've met were in fact super nice and polite, and some made me feel as if they could be the religious example for others to follow when it came to showing concern for others. Admitting this made me feel as if I was compromising my religious values, and I was starting to sound as if I was slowly beginning to accept their way of thinking. In fact, for some reason, I felt that I was supposed to react differently toward homosexuality than the way I'm actually reacting to it; and if I don't go against it, it indicates that I actually agree with what homosexuals do. This kind of thinking made me feel as if I had to be more conscious of what I was thinking and feeling. I wanted to be independent in my thinking in this matter, and I did not want to be influenced by anything other than what I chose to believe from information that I know were based on facts.

Choosing to look at homosexuality this way ignited a process within me that led to certain breakthroughs in my way of thinking. For the first time, I was not allowing myself to be influenced by religion or the things I learned before about homosexuality. I felt the need to try to love what I did not like. It was just like as a child—your parents trying to get you to taste food that you know you don't like but you need. Trying to learn to accept homosexuality was difficult, but it was absolutely necessary in my learning to humanize people's homosexuality. I had begun to see it as just simply being their God-given right of choice. This further served as my proof that it was a more productive way to address this subject, for myself and for others that I came in contact with. We may all have different experiences and beliefs. If we are adjusting our lives because of someone who is homosexual. By doing this, we all will face this challenge with or without knowledge on the subject. Nevertheless, there are similarities in all our struggles, and they begin first within our families. Each individual of our families have their unique way of seeing things differently, and we must all seek the appropriate ways to adapt to the homosexuality of our family and of others that are this way as well.

Finding out about someone's homosexuality is normally done with our family and friends. This process can either divide a family or relationship. I challenge those that do, to not give up in their pursuit to do as the Bible requires—that is, to do unto others as you would want others to do to you.

Afterword

I hope you enjoyed this book as much as I enjoyed writing it. After reading my book, I would much appreciate it if you would please go to the link www.Amazon.com/books. Type in the name of the book, *Torn Between My Love for God and Gays*, and provide a book review if you enjoyed the book.

Also, please follow me on Twitter (username: @AuthorJoeNBrown), and look for me or my book on Facebook. We appreciate the likes on our page.

Remember to also look up *Before the Beginning of Genesis* (www.beforethebeginningofgenesis.com). It is a book on theology regarding our spiritual creation, the war in heaven, Satan and the fallen angels, evolution, Jesus, and the biblical mysteries. Please look for my future books as well.

About the Author

Joe N. Brown Sr. is also the author of Amazon's best-selling book entitled, *Before the Beginning of Genesis,* which ranked number 5 in the Top 100 Religious and Spirituality books in July 2013 and made the *New York Times* in November 2013. (See www.beforethebeginningofgenesis.com.) Mr. Brown is a resident of Colorado Springs, Colorado and has been married for thirty-six years to his childhood sweetheart, Neecha Jackson-Brown. They have four children in their union, but they share a total of eight children altogether within their unification and are blessed with many healthy and happy grandchildren.

This author's experience in religion began as a preacher's son. His father's messages were heard by Mr. Brown from infancy throughout his adult life. This deeply rooted religious knowledge was learned by him from the influence of his family ministry. This author has had multiple interviews and conversations with religious leaders about homosexuality and other complex religious subjects. He has previously written other religious texts, which gives Joe N. Brown Sr. the gift of insight in being able to understand ambiguous and delicate issues in the religious studies of the Bible.

As a result of the author's close ties to his family and his religion, and after he later realized that his two sisters and other relatives were homosexuals, Mr. Brown felt that this was not only in conflict with his religious belief but was also in conflict with the love and respect that he held for his sisters and which he sought to maintain with them. The combination of Mr. Brown's religious experience, his experience from his relationship with homosexuals in his family, and the fact that Mr. Brown has made it his duty out of his passion for maintaining homosexual relationships of family and others that he knew is what gives him this unique experience. As a result of this, the author has supported and advocated the need for religious believers to accept everyone, regardless of who they are. The author maintains that this is the true concept of our expression of love and an example of what God's expectations are for those who love and follow God.

Printed in Poland
by Amazon Fulfillment
Poland Sp. z o.o., Wrocław